At Issue

Should the Internet Be Free?

D1297736

Other Books in the At Issue Series:

At Issue

Should the Internet Be Free?

Roman Espejo, Book Editor

GREENHAVEN PRESS
A part of Gale, Cengage Learning

Detroit • New York • San Francisco • New Haven, Conn • Waterville, Maine • London

Christine Nasso, *Publisher*
Elizabeth Des Chenes, *Managing Editor*

© 2010 Greenhaven Press, a part of Gale, Cengage Learning.

For more information, contact:
Greenhaven Press
27500 Drake Rd.
Farmington Hills, MI 48331-3535
Or you can visit our Internet site at gale.cengage.com

For product information and technology assistance, contact us at

Gale Customer Support, 1-800-877-4253
For permission to use material from this text or product, submit all requests online at
www.cengage.com/permissions

Further permissions questions can be e-mailed to permissionrequest@cengage.com

Articles in Greenhaven Press anthologies are often edited for length to meet page requirements. In addition, original titles of these works are changed to clearly present the main thesis and to explicitly indicate the author's opinion. Every effort is made to ensure that Greenhaven Press accurately reflects the original intent of the authors. Every effort has been made to trace the owners of copyrighted material.

Cover photograph reproduced by permission of Brand X Pictures.

LIBRARY OF CONGRESS CATALOGING-IN-PUBLICATION DATA

Should the Internet be free? / Roman Espejo, book editor.
        p. cm. -- (At issue)
    Includes bibliographical references and index.
    ISBN 978-0-7377-4687-7 (hardcover) -- ISBN 978-0-7377-4688-4 (pbk.)
    1. Internet. 2. Internet--Social aspects. 3. Broadband communication systems. I.
Espejo, Roman, 1977-
    TK5105.875.I57S5324 2010
    004.67'8--dc22

                                                                2009048056

Printed in the United States of America
1 2 3 4 5 6 7 14 13 12 11 10

Contents

Introduction

In the fall of 2004, the government of Philadelphia, Pa., announced it planned to build a free wireless broadband network that would cover all 135 square miles of the city. Several thousand transmitters—compatible with the wireless interface network cards found on most newer computers and laptops—would be installed from lamppost to lamppost across Philadelphia, using radio waves to deliver broadband. This would meet a critical need in poor neighborhoods, where most residents lacked high-speed Internet access. City officials estimated that it would cost $10 million, making the initiative one of the first and the largest of its kind in the country.

A year later, Philadelphia chose EarthLink, an Internet service provider (ISP) based in Atlanta to develop the municipal wireless network. No taxpayer money would be used to fund the project. EarthLink agreed to finance, build, and operate it; revenues would be created from allowing other ISPs to buy bandwidth on the network. In addition, Philadelphia residents could still choose and pay for their own ISPs, including Earth-Link. "We'll make [the network] available at very reasonable rates," said Cole Reinwand, then EarthLink's director of next-generation broadband. "We want to avoid any issue of over-building."[1]

Verizon, another major ISP, criticized Philadelphia's partnership with EarthLink. Responding to such concerns, Dianah Neff, former chief information officer of the city, said, "We have believed from the beginning that the nonprofit [Wireless Philadelphia, the nonprofit set up by the city] could take on the risk." She continued that "EarthLink stepping up and offering to fund this at their risk . . . was very important to us."[2] The wireless network was scheduled to be up and running by late 2006.

Building the municipal broadband network turned out to be much more complicated and costly than originally planned. EarthLink faced hurdles in installing the transmitters on lampposts, the technology of which proved to be unreliable and difficult to set up. Competition from other ISPs stifled subscribership to EarthLink. In May 2008, the company withdrew and looked to sell what had become a $17 million project. "It was a great idea a few years ago," said Rolla Huff, the company's chief executive officer, "but it's an idea that simply didn't make it."[3] Doug Oliver, spokesman for Philadelphia's mayor, offered a different take: "Now they say, 'We don't want to do it. We're walking away and we're taking our marbles.'"[4] At the point at which EarthLink abandoned the project, only about 20 to 30 percent coverage of the city had been built.

Philadelphia's ambitious plan to provide wireless broadband for all residents exemplifies the logistical issues and financial challenges of establishing a municipally provided network. Recognizing the socioeconomic advantages of high-speed Internet access, other cities in the United States tried to do the same, with mixed results. San Francisco also embarked on a municipal wireless network with EarthLink and Google in early 2007. The project folded, however, in August 2008 because a deteriorating customer base forced EarthLink to back out of all free Internet-access initiatives. The EarthLink project in Houston met the same fate. Budgets ballooned beyond expectations, as did the unanticipated need for more access points. For instance, Miami-Dade County's aim to build a 2,000-mile municipal broadband network was downgraded to provisional Wi-Fi hot spots in public parks. Miami-Dade County Mayor Carlos Alvarez claimed it was a "service that was economically and technically unfeasible."[5]

Still, other places have realized their goals of wireless-for-all. In March 2006, St. Cloud, Florida, began its municipal broadband service. The fiber-optic network in Bristol, Virginia, got the attention of the social and economic development think tank Intelligent Community Forum, which ranked it as one of the seven "most intelligent cities" in 2009 and 2010. Corpus Christi, Texas, another city that joined forces with EarthLink, bought back the network from the struggling ISP. The government of Green County, North Carolina, installed its own Wi-Fi network. And not all was lost with the Philadelphia project, either. In June 2008, local investors stepped forward to buy the network from EarthLink and continue the objective of bringing wireless broadband access to the entire city, with talks of supporting the service with advertising.

The steps toward municipal broadband access in the past decade reflect the changing role of the Internet from a high-tech novelty to a driver of economic growth and social mobility. Some advocates of free Internet access believe the Internet should be treated as a public service accessible to everyone. Detractors, on the other hand, allege that municipal wireless service would kill competition between ISPs and local governments are not prepared to launch such initiatives. These arguments and other related issues are examined in *At Issue: Should the Internet Be Free?*

Notes

1. Grant Gross, "Philadelphia Picks EarthLink for Wi-Fi," *PC World*, October 5, 2005.
2. ———, "Philadelphia Picks EarthLink for Wi-Fi," *PC World*, October 5, 2005.
3. Deborah Yao, "EarthLink to Pull the Plug on Wi-Fi in Philadelphia," Associated Press, May 13, 2008.
4. ———, "EarthLink to Pull the Plug on Wi-Fi in Philadelphia," Associated Press, May 13, 2008.
5. David S. Elliott, "Muni Wireless Fizzles," http://english/ohmynews.com, February 10, 2008.

1

The Internet Should Be Free

Sascha Meinrath

Sascha Meinrath is research director of the Wireless Future Program at the New America Foundation, a Washington, D.C.-based nonprofit and nonpartisan economic and social development think tank.

From primary education to public libraries, basic services are readily available in contemporary society. In the digital age, broadband access to the Internet is the most important of these. Still, despite its many documented benefits and minimal costs compared with the recent bailout of Wall Street firms or the Iraq war, free broadband access for everyone—wireless and wireline—is not available. Opportunities to advance this goal exist, including financial support for broadband buildouts and M2Z Networks' hopeful proposal to obtain a spectrum license to provide free connectivity. But a comprehensive solution is necessary to a build a free national network.

We live in a civil society—a place where primary education is freely available to all, where anyone can enjoy a walk through our public parks or down our sidewalks and freely drive through the streets. Libraries across the country loan out books for free—literature that you can read on a spring day in our parks or beneath the streetlights on main street on a warm summer's evening. You don't have to tip the firemen who show up at your house or pay for police protection—in a civil society, public safety is freely available to everyone.

Sascha Meinrath, "Life, Liberty and Connectivity for All," *Guardian [London]*, January 5, 2009. Reproduced by permission of Guardian News Service, LTD.

We enjoy myriad services and resources that we don't pay for each and every time we use them. Yet each of these key facets of contemporary society was part of a new social contract, often adopted only after years of battle and turmoil to overcome a prior status quo (from private fire and educational services to for-fee libraries and parks). Eventually, however, new models are seen to provide such an enormous benefit to the entire population that we're willing to invest in ideas that lift all boats. We realise that, as a society, each of us is better off when certain basic services are freely available to all.

We realize that, as a society, each of us is better off when certain basic services are freely available to all.

The Currency of the Information Age

At the dawn of the digital era, during this first decade of the 21st century, the most important new commodity is Internet access. A growing canon of research has documented the enormous benefits that accrue to those with broadband access (and the increasing detriments faced by those without it). Within many civil societies, in much the same way the agrarian revolution helped eliminate famine, the industrial revolution brought manufactured goods into everyone's lives and the computer era integrated machines (from laptops to PDAs [personal digital assistants] and cell phones to iPods [portable devices used to store and play audio files]) into our daily regimes, connectivity is the currency of the information age. A new social contract that includes connectivity for all is not a particularly expensive endeavour—free broadband for everyone for life would cost a tiny fraction of the cost of the Wall Street bail-out and far less than the expense of one year of our war in Iraq.

Today's politicians, from municipal representatives to [President] Barack Obama, are actively supporting broadband buildouts. Current debates over the economic stimulus package place nationwide Internet infrastructure development as a key component of the intervention. An optimal free broadband system would include both wireless (for mobility and cost efficiency) and wireline (for capacity and reliability) components. And, as it turns out, two proposals are currently pending that could make free broadband connectivity for life a reality.

The first is an innovative public interest obligation on licensed spectrum. Since we already own the public airwaves (over which everything from television signals to FM radio is broadcast), as landlords, we can set the rental conditions. Every time a mobile phone company, TV broadcaster or other entity receives a license from the Federal Communications Commission (FCC) it comes with conditions. Earlier this year [in 2009], the FCC auctioned off a small portion of the 700 MHz spectrum for $19.6bn [billion]. Sadly, of that sum, zero dollars went to support free broadband. But if a small portion of spectrum auction revenues had been earmarked for free broadband for all, we would already be well on our way toward universal connectivity.

In the US, we have an opportunity to implement broadband solutions that dramatically improve the lives of everyone living in the country.

Currently, a small piece of spectrum (2155–2175 MHz) is up for license, and the conditions being proposed include providing free broadband connectivity for everyone in the US. One company in particular, M2Z Networks, has been vocally advocating to license this piece of the public airwaves with this condition. However, M2Z faces fierce competition from telecom incumbents like T-mobile, and the plan is currently stalled at the FCC.

A Critical New Infrastructure

But financial support and spectrum licensure reforms are not enough on their own. A multi-faceted solution is needed. Fuel-efficiency and car-safety standards have helped shape today's national transportation grid, but the US had to make a major public investment in the infrastructure itself. Broadband poses a similar opportunity.

Building the 21st-Century Information Superhighway is a proposal synthesised by the New America Foundation in consultation with numerous interested parties that would create a national information superhighway, providing fibre capacity to cities, towns and rural areas throughout the US. At its core, the idea is very simple: each time we rip up, repave or build a road, we should also lay fibre infrastructure along that route that anyone can use. Over the next half-decade, this initiative would create a web of connectivity—a critical new infrastructure for the digital age. Across the country, communities, Internet service providers and municipalities are engaging in demand-side aggregation, but lack entree to affordable Internet access, a bottleneck that this proposal solves.

Residents in places like Philadelphia, Pennsylvania, and St. Cloud, Florida, already receive free broadband. Groups like Tribal Digital Village [a project funded by the Hewlett-Packard Company to provide network access to American Indian reservations] and the CUWiN [Champaign-Urbana Community Wireless Network, based in Illinois] Foundation have been building free networks to serve local communities for years. There are thousands of networks all around the globe providing free connectivity to participants. In the US, we have an opportunity to implement broadband solutions that dramatically improve the lives of everyone living in the country. The question, therefore, is whether this new [Obama] administration has the gumption to create a "broadband Apollo project" to maximise the potential and possibility of the information age.

2

The Internet Should Not Be Free

James Plummer

James Plummer is a research assistant for Telecom, Internet, and Information Policy Studies at the Cato Institute, a libertarian public policy organization.

The attempt of M2Z Networks to secure spectrum at no cost for "free" broadband is clouded by rhetoric: For the digital have-nots, the company supposedly promises to provide universal Internet access. In reality, most Americans do not view Internet access as essential, and subsidized broadband access would require "family-friendly" filters that censor political speech and ideas. M2Z's free broadband service would also be obsolete when completed—slower, in fact, than low-priced plans currently available to Americans. In the end, the company's proposal uses the pretext of "public interest" to wrangle valuable spectrum for their pay service.

This month [January 2008] sees the long-awaited Federal Communications Commission (FCC) auction of "beachfront" wireless spectrum in the 700MHz range to companies looking to provide broadband Internet services. But there's already a battle brewing concerning another chunk of spectrum. The disposition of the band from 2155—2175 MHz may ultimately be settled in the federal courts. According to the FCC, it is for "fixed and mobile services and designated for Ad-

James Plummer, "'Free' (Filtered) Broadband?" *techknowledge*, January 24, 2008. Republished with permission of *techknowledge*, conveyed through Copyright Clearance Center, Inc.

The Internet Should Not Be Free

vanced Wireless Services (AWS) use." But a firm called M2Z Networks wants the FCC to turn it over, free of any upfront charge.

So, who is M2Z and what does it want to do with this spectrum? M2Z is headed by former FCC Wireless Bureau staffer John Muleta and backed to the tune of $400 million by a consortium of Silicon Valley venture capitalists. M2Z proposes to use the spectrum to build a wireless broadband network and offer free-of-charge access to 95 percent of the country within 10 years.

M2Z first filed its proposal in May 2006, after waiting several years for an FCC decision on what to do with the frequencies. Although the FCC is supposed to issue timely responses to such petitions, it wasn't until August 31, 2007, that the FCC finally denied M2Z's petition and issued a Notice of Proposed Rulemaking seeking comment on possible permanent uses of the spectrum. M2Z then filed suit challenging the FCC's action in October [2007], and the case is currently wending its way through the federal court system.

Almost one-third of households see little point in having Internet access at home.

By dangling the promise of "free," "public interest" services in front of the FCC, the M2Z proposal parallels the widely touted and largely adopted proposal submitted to the FCC by now-defunct Frontline Wireless regarding the disposition of the 700MHz wavelengths. Such rhetoric has evidently become boilerplate for firms seeking to pay less than a market rate for the right to use spectrum.

The So-Called "Digital Divide"

To that end, M2Z has leaned heavily on rhetoric regarding the so-called "digital divide"—the fact that the richer you are, the more likely you are to have broadband access. The assumption is that broadband access is akin to indoor plumbing or telephone service, an essential good that no American home can do without. It is an assumption with little basis, though. A recent survey revealed that almost one-third of households see little point in having Internet access at home in the first place. It found that more than half of U.S. households have broadband services at home, up from virtually zero 10 years ago. Only 11 percent of the 29 percent with no home Internet access (that's 2.3 percent overall) cite the cost of access as a sticking point. M2Z wants to bridge this divide by using the spectrum to provide free-of-charge, advertiser-supported consumer broadband.

To further the "public interest," this free service would be hobbled by content filters that M2Z touts as "family-friendly." Unfortunately, M2Z has not specified whether or not the filters would screen out such things as "hate speech." Many Internet filter services do, but the "hate speech" moniker has been used as fig leaf to cover for the blocking of objectionable political content, such as pro-Second Amendment websites. M2Z's broadband vision is analogous to the present situation with broadcast television, where spectrum-subsidized broadcasters offer sanitized entertainment and circumscribed political debate relative to the more freewheeling cable and satellite providers.

Consumers may just ignore the chance to use free, slow, sanitized wireless.

Any such plan raises serious questions: Would M2Z tweak its filters to curry favor with the FCC commissioners who vote on whether or not it is meeting its obligations as the spectrum licensee? Current FCC chairman Kevin Martin has shown a sudden zeal for extending its regulatory power to cable television, and a similar impulse toward control can be found in other commissioners and possible future chairmen—

even if their specific agendas are different. Their subsidized, censored media could crowd out uncensored information and a true marketplace of ideas.

But some critics would say that even that scenario gives the M2Z plan too much credit. It would offer 384 kilobits per second [kbps] downstream and 128 kbps upstream within 10 years, which will be obsolete by the time the network is built. In some places, a three megabits per second connection already can be gotten for around $30 per month. AT&T is now offering 768 kbps DSL [digital subscriber line] in some areas for $15 per month, and Verizon has a 15 Mbps [megabytes per second] service (40 times faster than the M2Z plan) for $53/month. Even wireless networks are rolling out "3G" data networks that will be faster than 384 kbps. Consumers may just ignore the chance to use free, slow, sanitized wireless.

No Special Moral Claim

M2Z also wants to offer a pay service, with no filters and no advertising, which would offer faster speeds, with five percent of the revenue going to the FCC. This reveals the heart of the M2Z plan: Get a hold of spectrum by pitching a "free" service in "the public interest," then convert it to a for-profit network, using spectrum assets it otherwise would have had to buy.

Although M2Z has characterized the spectrum in question as "fallow," [dormant, or inactive] there are in fact several users on the frequencies which would have to be moved, at some cost. Mobile-radio and cell-phone networks use the wavelengths to move traffic within their network backbones, just not directly to consumers. Those services ultimately serve the public as well.

The M2Z business plan for subsidized, sanitized, "free" wireless Internet access simply has no special moral claim to the 2100MHz spectrum. M2Z is correct when it says that the notoriously inefficient FCC needs to stop playing games and decide once and for all what to do with the spectrum. But that's not for the sake of M2Z. Participants in this month's spectrum auction are not acting on complete information because they don't know when or if there will be another spectrum auction—or a giveaway—for another competitive consumer broadband offering.

3

Broadband Access Is Nearing a Shortage

Galen Gruman and Tom Kaneshige

Galen Gruman is executive editor of InfoWorld, *an online magazine for information technology, where Tom Kaneshige was a former senior writer.*

The "free ride" culture of the Internet may spell a bandwidth shortage in the near future. In the last few years, the exponential rise in video usage, file-downloading, business applications, and media-rich Web sites have doubled and tripled the demand for broadband, a shared resource. Because federal regulation is unlikely, it is only a matter of time when the telecommunications industry bases charges on consumer usage with tiered pricing and metered billing—some carriers already enforce caps for monthly downloads. These measures, however, are unpopular, and it is unfair to blame only consumers for using too much bandwidth. In addition, broadband providers could better use their available capacities and optimize their networks.

The digital Disneyland of the future—where we freely work and play online—may be at risk. Why? Because, some argue, broadband carriers can't support it. The Internet's "free ride" culture has led to more people downloading gigabytes of data at practically no cost. Even if broadband infrastructure's capacity doubled or tripled, there's no avoiding the equivalent of an abrupt work stoppage.

Galen Gruman and Tom Kaneshige, "Is Our Internet Future in Danger?" *InfoWorld.com*, November 11, 2008. Republished with permission of *InfoWorld*, conveyed through Copyright Clearance Center, Inc.

There are signs of the free ride being nearly over. In the U.K. [United Kingdom], a million users are about to bump into "soft caps" for usage that their carriers imposed, according to consumer research group uSwitch. In the U.S., some carriers have also started imposing caps that customers have found out about only when they exceeded them in their inaccurately labeled "unlimited" plans. (These limits were hidden in the "unlimited" contracts' fine print.) Comcast, for example, now has a national cap of 256GBs [gigabytes] per month. And a few are experimenting with tiered pricing, where the more you use, the more you pay—just like you do for electrical, gas, and water.

Where is all the bandwidth going? Downloading Iron Man in HD [high definition], tapping cloud-computing services for business purposes, deploying collaboration technologies that connect disparate workforces, downloading and sharing music and other entertainment files, playing online games, and using remote-work tools like VPNs [virtual private network], VoIP [voice-over Internet protocol], and app [application] streaming.

"In the space of two, three years, [bandwidth] demand has been doubling and tripling," says Michael Voellinger, senior vice president at Telwares, which helps clients manage telecommunications spending. "And there's only a certain amount of capacity. It's a shared resource."

To be fair, some analysts say there is no bandwidth crisis looming, that there is plenty of capacity available. Derek Turner, research director of the anti-"big media" advocacy group Free Press, says if there were a looming shortage, most carriers would have already imposed tiered pricing or explicit caps; the fact that only a few do points to weaknesses in their specific infrastructure, not to a general shortage of capacity.

But assuming a looming bandwidth shortage—whether widespread or local to certain areas—analysts agree that two things must change. First, bandwidth pricing needs to be like any other precious utility, such as water or electricity, which means charging heavy users more to both discourage wasteful usage and bring in money to support such usage. "Broadband is becoming a utility" with a baseline usage cost and overage charges, says Gartner [an information technology research and advisory firm headquartered in Stamford, Connecticut] analyst Elroy Jopling. "You wouldn't leave the faucet on and let it run." Second, service and content providers need to rework their networks, protocols, and content to use less bandwidth.

Short of the federal government stepping in—an unlikely event given historic U.S. aversion to regulation—the telecom industry will likely adopt its own approach, focusing on increasing revenues from its customers or limiting their use through pricing penalties.

As video is increasingly downloaded over the Internet, carriers could see their customers' bandwidth usage quadruple or more.

Video Usage Could Bring Us to the Breaking Point

The main culprit today for high-bandwidth usage is video, both user-generated and commercially available. Carriers underestimated the growth in video usage, says Forrester Research [a technology and market research company] analyst Lisa Pierce, who cites an AT&T claim that video counts for 40 percent of the Internet traffic it carries—up from almost none three years ago. An AT&T spokesperson says that 5 percent of its subscribers account for half its broadband traffic usage, and cites those heavy users as why it's exploring new pricing models.

It's easy to miss how much media services eat up bandwidth. So Gartner analyst Jopling has come up with a rough consumption guide for what his provider's 96GB monthly usage cap supports: 32 hours of interactive gaming, or 48,000 photos, or 900,000 e-mails, or 24 HD movie downloads. Downloading a single high-definition movie eats up 4GB to 5GB, which also happens to be the total amount of data that the average broadband subscriber downloads in a month.

As video is increasingly downloaded over the Internet, carriers could see their customers' bandwidth usage quadruple or more. Video providers are egging customers on: Amazon.com, Blockbuster Video, and Netflix now all offer various movie-download services, including options that stream videos straight to TiVo digital video recorders. To customers, these are simply convenient delivery options; the fact that they consume so much bandwidth is rarely considered.

And today's 10- to 22-year-olds will push the envelope even further, notes Gartner analyst Amanda Sabia. In several focus groups she has run, this cohort says it expects to use video even more than today's typical user but expects to pay no more for the bandwidth. Forrester's Pierce agrees the bandwidth-consumption problem is only going to get worse as next-generation students make their way into companies. They've been weaned on the idea that video, music, and gaming are essentially free and unlimited, and thus act accordingly. "Students live in very wired areas," Pierce says, "which is great for education, but it's not the real world."

The real issue is not video, but the ever-increasing use of the Internet for content and services that take more and more bits each generation, notes Pierce. "What is 'high usage' will be a moving target for the rest of our lives," she adds. For example, Facebook traffic represents about 10 percent of the total Internet usage, she notes. Then there's the plethora of YouTube videos, online gaming, multimedia-rich sites like Disney, and sites like ESPN that automatically launch videos when people visit them, all consuming massive chunks of bandwidth capacity.

"I am concerned that we're seeing a lot of stuff from Web sites being incredibly, overly rich," says Jack Wilson, enterprise architect at Amerisure Insurance, which has a large remote workforce dependent on residential broadband service to do their jobs. "It can even be a problem inside the network. Half a dozen people streaming audio could cause a big bump in our pipe even to one of our remote locations, even to a T1 line."

Contributing to the problem is how content is distributed. For example, peer-to-peer traffic—whether to share videos, game-playing, or music—is very inefficient compared to streaming content from a single provider, notes Pierce. The reason is that the network architectures weren't designed for peer-to-peer, which assumes as much bandwidth in each direction, while broadband networks give most of their bandwidth to downloading. That means the uploading channel gets clogged much faster, and the downloading channel may sit empty waiting for the upload to complete.

It's no secret that Americans' appetite for broadband has been enormous ever since cable and DSL service appeared on the menu only a few years ago.

That's why Japan's telecom ministry is investigating a rearchitecting of its broadband network to work better with peer-to-peer traffic—emerging peer-to-peer protocols may actually make that sort of traffic more efficient than traditional traffic on such a rearchitected network. But such a rearchitecture effort will be costly and take many years, so even if it is a better model, it won't be in place any time soon, Pierce says.

Companies are also adding to the capacity problem, although not on the scale of video. Many allow more and more employees to work from home, whether periodically or full-time. Remote tools such as VoIP, VPNs, and most notably, videoconferencing, consume bandwidth at little or no cost to the company. Such services don't consume nearly as much bandwidth as video, and the current broadband infrastructure could handle them, notes Gartner analyst Jopling. But video and future bandwidth hogs could get in the way of such services' availability. "It's unrealistic to have all entertainment be delivered digitally [over the Internet]," he says. "You would need fiber to the home [everywhere] to be able to have unlimited capacity."

The Pressures Against Increasing Capacity

It's no secret that Americans' appetite for broadband has been enormous ever since cable and DSL [digital subscriber line] service appeared on the menu only a few years ago. Today, more than half of adult Americans have broadband at home, with nearly a third subscribing to a premium broadband service that gives them a faster Internet connection, according to a recent survey by Pew Internet and American Life Project.

The top 20 cable and telephone providers—such as Comcast, Cox, and Time Warner for cable, as well as AT&T, Qwest, and Verizon for telecom—boast nearly 65 million subscribers, representing about 94 percent of the U.S. market, Leichtman Research Group reports.

With that level of penetration, the carriers are now moving to open up the pipelines. Verizon, for instance, is investing $23 billion to roll out by 2010 in many parts of the country its FiOS fiber-optic network, which provides Internet, television, and telephone service at near-100Mbps [megabytes per second] download speeds. Meanwhile, AT&T is spending $4.6 billion to upgrade its network with fiber optics.

Broadband cable providers are also trying to open the pipe. A technology called wideband, whereby cable operators bond several channels together to increase Internet-access speeds, is gaining momentum. This technique can provide speeds of 150Mbps.

But such large investments have been slow in coming, mainly because Wall Street dislikes them. Every dollar on capital improvements reduces carriers' profits, and investors tend to punish capital investments by reducing carriers' stock prices, notes the Free Press's Turner. Because most broadband providers have little or no competition, he says, the Wall Street pressure usually prevails.

Here Come Usage Caps, Overage Charges, and Metered Internet

Despite the distaste for capital investment, carriers have begun investing in it. A big reason is that with the high availability of broadband in urban and suburban areas, there aren't enough profitable new customers left to reach.

Carriers can't raise prices for their current service levels—current prices are already too high to attract the broadband holdouts. But the carriers also can't lower their prices to attract those customers, since that would reduce their income as existing customers trade down to lower-priced plans, says Gartner's Jopling. "For the foreseeable future, there is a limit on how pricing may increase or decrease. We will only get much lower prices if every home has fiber to it," because that would make capacity essentially unlimited.

That leaves two options: offering premium-priced high-capacity services (a form of tiered pricing) and charging based on usage. Carriers are experimenting with both to bring in more dollars.

Usage caps are the stealth form of usage-based pricing, though several lawsuits have forced U.S. carriers to stop being secretive about them. For example, Comcast agreed this summer to pay Florida $150,000 in a settlement over Comcast's policy of prohibiting excessive use of bandwidth without informing customers of limits. Some customers had their service cut off. In October, Comcast started its new policy, which limits the amount of data a subscriber can send and receive every month at 250GB. Violators will have their service suspended for a year.

Now, Time Warner Cable is testing metered-usage pricing. New broadband subscribers in Beaumont, Texas, are the test case. Pricing starts at $29.95 a month for a speed of 768Kbps [kilobytes per second] and a 5GB usage cap, and it goes up to $54.90 for 15Mbps speed and a 40GB cap. It costs $1 for every gigabyte of usage over the cap. Subscribers can check their usage on Time Warner Cable's Web page. AT&T is testing a similar plan in Reno [Nevada]; the basic $15 768Kbps plan has a 20GB-per-month usage cap, while the as-yet-unpriced 10Mbps plan has a 150GB-per-month usage cap. Users pay $1 per extra gigabyte used, and can check their usage at AT&T's Web site.

But metered billing has quickly come under fire. AOL tried metered billing in the early days of the Internet, and consumers ultimately rejected it; AOL introduced an unlimited usage plan in 1996.

As Time Warner Cable turns back the clock, Free Press's Turner complains, "Its overage fees with rates are completely divorced from what it actually costs Time Warner to provide that data. I don't think you'll see a shift to caps and overage fees—consumers really don't like surprise bills." Agrees Telwares's Voellinger: "A cap isn't the answer to this. You don't want to limit what people can do."

Broadband and Service Providers Need to Be More Efficient

It's easy to blame consumers for overusing bandwidth, but it's unfair to single them out.

Consumers do in fact pay for the bandwidth they use, at least partially, notes Free Press's Turner. Content providers pay their Web hosts (or dedicated Internet providers if they host their own Web servers) based on the traffic they use, so customers pay them based on usage. Thus, a video provider pays more to serve up its offerings than a simple Web site does. And this usage-based money moves throughout the broadband ecosystem, with each Web host paying its dedicated Internet provider based on usage, each dedicated Internet provider paying the backbone providers based on usage, and each backbone provider paying the intermediate and last-mile providers based on usage. Even if a content provider like Facebook doesn't charge its customers directly, it is paying for the traffic they use through the fees it pays directly and indirectly to all the infrastructure providers between it and those customers.

However, such indirect payments to the carriers don't foot enough of the bill, says Forrester's Pierce. The providers pay for the bandwidth of what they put into the Internet, but because content and services are used repeatedly, that upfront loading cost represents just a fraction of the downstream consuming cost. For example, if Netflix or Apple uploads a video, it pays for the traffic for that single upload, not for the multiple downloads by users, she notes. That's why carriers are increasingly focused on charging users for their consumption.

A carrier that underinvests in capacity or is inefficient in its network management becomes a bottleneck for all the Internet traffic that passes through it.

Pierce suggests that content providers should pay more upfront, building the cost into their pricing. She notes that's exactly how Amazon.com's Kindle e-book reader service works: Amazon.com pays Sprint a fee for every e-book sold, since Sprint delivers the content to Kindles over its 3G cellular network. Such a deal was fairly straightforward in the Kindle case, she acknowledges, because only Sprint's network is involved. But Pierce suggests that the same approach could be adapted to the existing system in which content providers indirectly pay carriers for traffic through their Web hosts and dedicated Internet providers. This approach would also have the advantage of allocating the costs to those who actually consume the content.

Regardless of how the usage costs are apportioned, the broadband providers could do much more to better use the capacity they already have, Telware's Voellinger says: "What I see is a need for better optimization of the provider network and broader delivery of broadband capacity. There's room in the bandwidth right now to do a lot more." Forrester's Pierce agrees, noting the carriers are very "uneven" in their network-management capabilities. Because the Internet is a shared network, a carrier that underinvests in capacity or is inefficient in its network management becomes a bottleneck for all the Internet traffic that passes through it. And Internet traffic passes through dozens if not hundreds of networks on its way to the user, so the chances of hitting a bottlenecked segment is fairly high. "To get the best experience, you need to look at the weakest link," she says.

"IP [Internet protocol] traffic is notoriously unpredictable versus ATM and frame relay [data transmission techniques in computer networking]," says Forrester's Pierce. So carriers reserve 50 percent of the capacity for peak burst traffic over IP, she says, compared with 30 percent for frame relay. The use of network-management technology would help broadband providers reduce the amount of capacity left "dark" for peak usage, Pierce adds. She believes tiered pricing would make Internet usage more predictable, also helping providers hedge their capacity less and thus free up existing capacity.

4

Broadband Access Is Not Nearing a Shortage

Ryan H. Sager

Ryan H. Sager is a reporter for Reason *magazine's Washington, D.C., office.*

Although the demand for and frenzy over broadband access continues to grow, there is no shortage. According to Sager, pricing and not access is the issue with broadband and the government should not interfere with regulations. Certain Internet service providers (ISPs) such as America Online (AOL) believe that the broadband market is limited and ISPs should be forced by the government to open their broadband markets to other providers. According to the following article, the broadband market is much healthier than open access supporters would have the public believe.

"Open access" regulations may delay faster Internet connections.

In the last few years AT&T has spent more than $100 billion building a broadband cable network capable of providing high-speed Internet access and local telephone services along with TV programming. Given such a bundle of services and the Internet's stunningly steep adoption curve, AT&T is hoping that consumers will sign up in droves. It figures that by getting out in the field first, it should be able to snag the lion's share of the nation's cable modem users.

The trade publication *Cable Datacom News* estimates that there are currently about 1.5 million such customers in the U.S. and Canada, a figure it estimates will be 15.9 million by 2003. It's hard to overstate the growing frenzy over broadband, since the technology allows users to access the Internet at speeds unimaginable with even the best 56K modem connection and is seen as crucial to the future of Web-based business.

But even if broadband is the next big thing, it's not clear yet if and when AT&T's bet will pay off in full. The company's Excite@Home service, which offers a cable modem and full Internet access for about $45 a month, has about 600,000 subscribers. But *The Wall Street Journal* and others have cast a cold eye on AT&T's cable and Internet operations, accusing them of underperforming and blaming them for the telecom giant's recent earnings woes.

If the vagaries of the marketplace aren't enough to deal with, AT&T has also picked up a few hitchhikers on its own information superhighway. Internet service providers (ISPs) such as America Online [AOL], Mindspring, and Erols are trying to catch a ride on AT&T's "fat pipe." These ISPs, which present themselves as "open access" advocates, are lobbying the Federal Communications Commission [FCC] to force AT&T and other cable companies to lease them space on their super fast systems at cut-rate, regulated prices.

Pricing Is the Critical Issue

Pricing, not access per se, is the critical issue. Currently, most cable-based broadband providers have exclusive contracts with their own ISPs, such as Excite@Home and Time Warner's RoadRunner. When those deals expire—AT&T's runs out in 2002, for example—it's generally accepted that broadband providers will start leasing space at market rates to competing ISPs. The only question is how much it's going to cost.

Abetting the ISPs in the battle for open access are self-styled consumer advocates. The advocates claim that AT&T and other cable companies offering similar services possess an illegal monopoly and should be forced to open their systems to competitors at below-market rates. This is not a stupid argument on its face. After all, the cable companies are themselves creatures of government, built on municipally granted exclusive franchises. But the investment in broadband, like the development of the technology itself, has been market-driven, and any policy that substantially reduces the potential return is likely to slow implementation and stifle innovation. After all, why take the risks if you can't get the rewards?

Most people would agree that the preferred regulatory regime is the one most likely to provide customers with the broadest range of services and options—a criterion that undercuts the open-access position. Nothing, however, is settled, and how this battle plays out over the next few years will have a serious impact on how quickly the average American can expect to get high-speed access to the Internet. It's also an object lesson in how consumer advocates are often a consumer's worst friends.

So far, the open access crowd has found little sympathy in the nation's capital. The FCC has prudently refused to step in and regulate an industry that has barely taken shape. But a series of orchestrated local battles has already yielded some results for AOL and its allies, as they have been able to convince a handful of municipalities to implement a policy that the feds have rejected.

In early June, Portland, Oregon, became the first city to require AT&T to open its cable network to competing ISPs. AT&T promptly filed suit, but the city's decision was upheld by a federal court, and an appeal to the U.S. Court of Appeals for the 9th Circuit is pending. Other localities have ordered AT&T's pipe opened up, including Broward County in Florida, and Cambridge and Weymouth in Massachusetts. St. Louis

[Mo.] has taken preliminary steps toward open access. In October, the city of Fairfax, Virginia, required its cable provider, Atlanta-based Cox Communications, to open up its network. Cox has so far threatened to sue the city and to refuse to provide Internet service there. (Additionally, as of press time in mid-November, a group of lawyers in Los Angeles were seeking certification of a federal class-action lawsuit against several cable companies, claiming some 500,000 consumers were being overcharged for or denied broadband access.)

The strategy of fighting local battles in the absence of federal support for open access was the brainchild of George Vradenburg III, AOL's senior vice president for global and strategic policy. A Hollywood lawyer brought in by an AOL desperate to find its home in the broadband market, Vradenburg is a shrewd tactician and a friend of such Washington notables as David Boies, the lead attorney in the Department of Justice's antitrust case against Microsoft. In November 1998, Vradenburg created the openNet Coalition, a lobbying group made up of ISPs threatened by AT&T's burgeoning high-speed capabilities. Reporting on a meeting put together by Vradenburg at Washington's Willard Hotel, *Regardie's Power*, a D.C. business magazine, outlined the group's basic strategy: to attack AT&T in the name of consumer choice.

But the open access lobby's initial bid to curry regulatory favor with the FCC failed miserably. Essentially, commissioners didn't buy AOL's claim of being shut out of the broadband market, especially since the world's biggest ISP was simultaneously cutting deals with local phone companies and satellite carriers to provide broadband access via non-cable means. Faced with a Republican Congress not likely to be sympathetic to its cause, AOL instead has taken its case to local city councils—a strategy that has AT&T hopping mad.

"It isn't the role of government to step in and force cable companies to open up their pipes to other ISPs," says Jim McGann of AT&T's government affairs office in Washington,

D.C. "We are perfectly willing to sit down with AOL or other ISPs and negotiate access on business terms." That is, of course, after AT&T's exclusive deal with Excite@Home expires. Until then, AT&T's clear message is that it will not be giving anyone access at any price, as per its contract with Excite@Home.

With the FCC solidly on its side, AT&T has little reason to negotiate. At every step so far, the FCC has supported AT&T's entry into the cable and broadband markets, even relaxing federal cable ownership restrictions in October to clear the way for AT&T's acquisition of cable operator MediaOne. FCC Chairman William Kennard has looked favorably on AT&T's expansion, at least in part because of the competition that he sees AT&T as able to bring to the local telephone market. He also does not see the broadband market as in any way monopolized, citing satellite services such as Hughes Network Systems' DirecPC and phone-line-based technologies such as Digital Subscriber Line (DSL), both of which provide competition to cable.

Broadband and the Prices of Internet Connections

"We don't . . . have a monopoly in broadband," Kennard told a group of communications lawyers in San Francisco in July. "We have a 'no-opoly.'" Kennard sees it as simply too early to regulate, stressing that "the bottom line is that most Americans don't even have [access to] broadband."

Contrary to the claims of open access advocates, the broadband market is in fact robust with prices falling and services improving.

That is expected to change in the near future, of course, which is precisely why there is such a large battle brewing now. By investing so heavily now, AT&T has managed to capture a good portion of early adopters. But whether it will be able to hold on to—much less expand—its customer base remains to be seen.

Steve Cohen, a spokesman for the openNet Coalition, emphatically denies that there's choice available in broadband access, saying, "I think the consumer should have the same freedom of choice and opportunity that they have right now with dial-up" Internet access. While such rhetoric pushes the right consumer buttons, it ignores Kennard's trenchant observation: While most Americans don't have broadband access, there is a growing range of options in the marketplace.

There are also wholly wireless ways to get broadband access.

Though open access proponents discount non-cable-based broadband methods, many of these technologies are making significant inroads. DSL—a broadband technology that can run over upgraded traditional copper wires—used to be an expensive alternative but has come down significantly in price. U.S. West, a regional Bell operating in 14 Western states, now offers DSL Internet access for as low as $20 a month. The highest speeds cost more (about $40 a month), but even the slowest DSL is three times faster than a conventional 56K dial-up modem. In July, there were about 92,000 DSL subscribers in the U.S. That number is expected to rise dramatically over the next three years. Spurred by the threat of cable modems, all the Baby Bells have announced plans to start selling DSL, and industry analysts predict that there will be roughly 94 million DSL lines available by 2002.

Wireless Broadband Access and Varying Prices

There are also wholly wireless ways to get broadband access. "Terrestrial wireless," similar to cellular phone networks, is an idea that is actively being pursued by companies such as Sprint and Motorola. Sprint has already started offering a terrestrial wireless "Integrated On-Demand Network," which provides voice, broadband Internet, and video. Motorola and Sun Microsystems are teaming up to invest $1 billion in infrastructure for wireless digital networks with similar capabilities. Both of these ventures will at first be aimed at small and medium businesses but are expected to be available to residential customers within five years.

Aside from terrestrial wireless, there is also satellite. Comparable in price to DSL and similar to TV services such as DISH Network and DirecTV, satellite services offer residential consumers who have room for a mini-satellite dish access to the Internet at eight times the speed of a traditional modem. At this point, the dishes cost around $250, though prices are dropping regularly. Monthly service fees start around $20 and increase based on usage.

Not only are these wireless technologies viable, but for rural markets they are often the only choice. Cable tends to have weak or nonexistent market share in rural areas, and even DSL is unavailable to customers more than 18,000 feet away from a telephone company central office. Indeed, wireless technologies are so attractive that AOL has invested heavily in both, making a $1.5 billion deal with satellite provider Hughes Electronics Corp. and entering into partnerships with Bell Atlantic and SBC Communications.

Broadband Access Is Robust

So, contrary to the claims of open access advocates, the broadband market is in fact robust with prices falling and services improving. In fact, about the only thing that could go wrong at this point would be for excessive new regulations to stunt the growth of this promising new sector of the economy.

Lawrence Gasman, president of Communications Industry Researchers, a consulting firm that assesses the commercial impact of new information technologies, sees regulation as a potential disaster that would discourage investment in new and competing technologies. He points out that there are a number of unresolved issues on the technological side. No one, he says, is quite certain if the technology exists to allow more than one ISP to share the same network, and there are large questions regarding network administration. While Gasman stresses that these questions will be answered, he suggests that ham-handed regulations of access and pricing will slow down development of broadband.

The most sensible policy in this area is to leave the market to progress on its own.

"If you tell a cable or a Bell company that on top of all the problems they're having implementing a new system, they're going to have to deal with opening it to anyone else— that might be a real discouragement to creating a network in the first place,"says Gasman. "The concern that there won't be enough competition is misplaced. If there's no network, there's no competition."

If the argument sounds far-fetched, it isn't. AT&T has already made it clear that those cities which impose burdensome open access requirements will be the last to see broadband. The company is not simply being vindictive, but recognizing that it will not make as much money in cities where other ISPs have a claim to the networks it is building.

It Is Better to Leave the Government out of the Broadband Market

As the FCC has argued in an amicus brief on behalf of AT&T in the case before the 9th Circuit, the most sensible policy in this area is to leave the market to progress on its own. Local control could only wreak havoc on an important framework that is just now developing. Maximum investment in broadband only will come when companies interested in investing in this technology can be assured that they will retain the rights to the networks they are creating.

That's especially true since, at this point, no broadband technology is truly dominant. Cable seems to have the lead for now, but billions of dollars are being poured into competing formats precisely because what will dominate is far from clear. AOL and the other ISPs in the openNet Coalition, then, haven't been shut out of the broadband market. They just dislike how much it's currently costing them to enter it. But in lobbying local governments to grab a share of the broadband pipe rather than getting on with the actual building of it, open access advocates may be slowing down the one thing they profess to care about most.

5

More Americans Have Broadband Internet Access

National Telecommunications and Information Administration

Part of the U.S. Department of Commerce, the National Telecommunications and Information Administration (NTIA) is the federal agency that specializes in telecommunications and information policies.

Under the administration of former President George W. Bush, more Americans than ever have broadband Internet access. Technology policies supporting competition, deregulation, and financial incentives have created a robust marketplace of Internet providers, increasing broadband availability and subscriptions in the United States. From high-speed cable to mobile wireless to fiber optics, the total number of broadband lines has increased 1,100 percent since December 2000, and usage in both urban and rural households has grown dramatically. Industry investment to maintain and improve the broadband network infrastructure is projected to rise, and increased competition among providers has kept service plans affordable.

Broadband technology is changing our lives, our economy, and our culture. By making it possible to access, use, and share information, news, and entertainment with ever increasing speed, broadband knits geographically distant individuals and businesses more closely together, increases our productivity, and enriches our quality of life. In so doing, it fuels eco-

National Telecommunications and Information Administration, "Networked Nation: Broadband in America 2007: Executive Summary," pp. i–iv, January 2008.

nomic growth and job creation that, in turn, provide unparalleled new opportunities for our nation's citizens.

Recognizing this transformative power, four years ago [in 2003] President [George W.] Bush articulated a national vision: universal, affordable access to broadband technology. From its first days, the Administration has implemented a comprehensive and integrated package of technology, regulatory, and fiscal policies designed to lower barriers and create an environment in which broadband innovation and competition can flourish.

The results have been striking. The last several years [pre 2007] have witnessed substantial growth in the broadband marketplace punctuated by increases in capital investment, innovation, and market entry. Relative to other countries, the United States has experienced superior productivity over the past several years. Americans today enjoy an increasing array of broadband services, available from a growing number of service providers, rising a variety of technologies. Penetration continues to grow, and prices continue to fall.

A Broadband Strategy for the Twenty-First Century

Building on the pro-competitive, deregulatory policies Congress articulated in the Telecommunications Act of 1996, the Administration, through the combined efforts of the National Telecommunications and Information Administration (NTIA) of the U.S. Department of Commerce, the U.S. Department of Agriculture (USDA), and other agencies, and in cooperation with the Federal Communications Commission (FCC or Commission), has executed a combination of initiatives to develop and rapidly deploy new technologies, eliminate regulatory underbrush, and remove economic disincentives for investment in this critical area.

Technology Policies. Technology Neutrality: Past experience teaches that when government tries to substitute its judgment for that of the market by favoring one product or vendor over another, it can easily divert investment and/or discourage research necessary to bring new and better products or services to market. Given the rapid pace of technological change, such unintended effects can have long-term and far-reaching adverse consequences that extend across multiple sectors of the economy. For this reason, the Administration has consistently and strenuously advocated for technology neutrality in order to take the government out of decisions more appropriately left to the marketplace.

Americans today enjoy an increasing array of broadband services.

Spectrum Policy: To satisfy society's increasing desire to function "untethered," new wireless broadband services can only emerge if spectrum resources exist to support them. Pursuant to the President's June 2003 Spectrum Policy Initiative, NTIA has promoted greater access to spectrum by improving the spectrum efficiency of Federal radio systems and operations. NTIA and the FCC, working together and with the Congress, have significantly increased the amount of spectrum available for advanced wireless services. The Administration has also actively sought ways to accelerate broadband deployment by facilitating unlicensed uses and encouraging the use of promising new spectrum technologies such as ultrawideband, and by implementing new spectrum management systems that afford non-Federal users faster and easier access to spectrum.

Regulatory Policies. The Administration has worked to clear away regulatory obstacles that could thwart the investment that fuels development—and deployment—of new technologies. It supported the FCC's efforts to modify legacy regulation in order to expand incentives for local telephone companies to invest in network upgrades and to stimulate facilities-based investments by other providers. The Administration has further encouraged aggressive broadband deployment by favoring policies to ensure that applications running on the Internet, such as voice over Internet Protocol service, remain free from unnecessary economic regulation. The Administration has also supported cable franchise reform efforts in order to promote the video services competition that will help to accelerate broadband deployment. In April 2004, the President signed an Executive Memorandum to give broadband providers more timely and cost-effective access to rights-of-way on Federal lands for their networks.

Fiscal Policies and Targeted Funding Efforts. Tax relief has given businesses powerful incentives to invest in broadband technology. Recognizing that taxes constrain growth, President Bush on three occasions has signed legislation to extend the Federal moratorium on State and local taxation of Internet access and has consistently urged that the moratorium be made permanent. The President also signed into law legislation allowing companies to accelerate depreciation for capital expenditures, including those associated with broadband deployment. The Administration has also forcefully advocated extending and making permanent the tax credit for research and development spending. Further, the Administration has provided targeted seed-funding to support more rapid deployment of broadband in underserved rural areas, in particular through several programs administered by the USDA.

Home broadband usage has risen substantially over the past six years, from 9.1 percent of households in September 2001 to 50.8 percent in October 2007.

Progress in Broadband Access

America's consumers are now reaping the rewards of the Administration's pro-investment, deregulatory policies: a vigorous broadband marketplace in which providers using various platforms compete against one another on price, speed, mobility, content, and other service features. Currently available data suggest that broadband availability and subscribership have increased dramatically, and that consumers—including those in rural and remote areas—have more opportunities than ever to choose the broadband solution (*i.e.*, technology, services, and provider) that best suits their needs and budget.

Overall. Since President Bush took office, the total number of broadband lines in the United States has grown by over 1,100 percent from almost 6.8 million lines in December 2000, to 82.5 million in December 2006 according to the most recent FCC data. Over 58 million of these lines serve residential customers. FCC data also reveal that the number of broadband service providers more than tripled from December 2003 to December 2006, with the newest wired and wireless services growing at the highest rates. Data from the U.S. Census Bureau's Internet Use Supplement to the October 2007 Current Population Survey also show that Americans' use of broadband technologies has soared: home broadband usage has risen substantially over the past six years, from 9.1 percent of households in September 2001 to 50.8 percent in October 2007. Rural America has also experienced impressive growth from 5.6 percent of rural households in September 2001 to 38.8 percent in October 2007.

Digital Subscriber Line (DSL). Used primarily by local telephone companies to provide broadband services, DSL was available as of year end 2006 to 79 percent of households in areas where companies also offered local telephone service according to FCC data. Not limited to highly populated areas, DSL was among the broadband services offered to 90 percent of the carriers' rural customer base according to recent industry surveys. As DSL transmission speeds have accelerated and prices have dropped, the number of DSL subscribers has burgeoned. FCC's statistics reveal about 22.8 million residential "high-speed" asymmetric DSL (ADSL) lines in service as of year end 2006, growing by more than 300 percent from December 2002.

High-Speed Cable. Research conducted by the cable television industry suggests that high-speed cable service is now available to some 92 percent of all U.S. households by the end of 2007. That same research shows that as of year end 2006, there were 29 million residential high-speed cable subscribers, up more than 109 percent from the 13.8 million customers in the second quarter of 2003. Accompanying this growth, the industry's trade association reports that most cable broadband operators now offer transmission speeds exceeding five megabits per second (5 Mbps), with some delivering as much as 50 Mbps.

Mobile Wireless. The wireless industry is currently the fastest growing segment of America's broadband economy. The FCC's most recent data reveal that the number of broadband lines provided by wireless operators increased from approximately 380,000 in June 2005 to almost 22 million at year end 2006—a growth rate that dwarfs that of other broadband platforms. Moreover, a significant portion of these (4.1 million, or almost 19 percent) provide "advanced" services capable of delivering over 200 kilobits per second (Kbps) in both directions.

Fixed Wireless. Fixed wireless technologies have emerged both as an important complement to mobile wireless and as a potential "last-mile" broadband solution in areas that other platforms do not reach. According to FCC figures, the number of fixed wireless broadband lines in the United States grew 132 percent from 208,695 in June 2005 to 484,073 in December 2006; an industry group estimated the total number of fixed wireless subscribers in 2006 to be 800,000. The proliferation of one fixed wireless technology—wireless fidelity (Wi-Fi)—

has increasingly enabled many consumers to cut the tether to a home or office connection; based on one estimate, there are 66,058 public/commercial Wi-Fi access points, or "hot spots", currently in the United States, more than double the next closest country. Another technology—worldwide interoperability for microwave access (WiMAX)—can deliver fixed wireless broadband access at distances as great as five miles without line of sight and up to 30 miles under ideal conditions. With potential data speeds up to 70 Mbps, WiMAX has been identified as a possible "last-mile" solution to deliver broadband into currently unserved rural and remote areas.

Satellite. With coverage of virtually the entire continent, satellite has become the default solution for areas not covered by terrestrial sources of broadband. Like those other broadband services, satellite broadband has seen tremendous growth over the past few years. From fewer than 50,000 subscribers in 2004, satellite providers were serving an estimated 700,000 subscribers at year end 2006.

Despite the dramatic increase in usage, the average local monthly bill for wireless services has remained relatively stable.

Fiber Optic and Broadband over Power Lines. FCC data show that the total number of high-speed lines delivered over fiber and power line connections grew 789 percent from December 2003 to December 2006, rising from 116,390 to just over a million. Fiber optic lines, however, appear to be almost entirely responsible for this expansion. Industry data also show a steady expansion of fiber deployment (including fiber to the home and interoffice fiber). As charted by the Telecommunications Industry Association (TIA), annual deployment of fiber in the United States grew sharply over the last four years, from the 4.8 million miles deployed in 2003 to 13.1 million miles in 2007. According to another industry estimate, fiber now passes almost 9.6 million homes in North America (virtually all of these homes are in the United States), up more than 50 percent from September 2006.

Industry Investment. The accessibility of broadband technology to an increasing number of Americans stems directly from the substantial and growing capital investments made by service providers across all of the subsectors of the broadband marketplace. TIA estimates that overall spending to support broadband network infrastructure will rise over the next four years from $15.2 billion in 2007 to $23 billion in 2010. This includes significant growth in fiber deployment by cable operators to meet customer demand for high-definition television channels and video-on-demand services; continued investment for the deployment of advanced mobile wireless services and fixed wireless technologies such as WiMAX; and spending on fiber-related telecommunications equipment that is estimated to grow almost $13.5 billion annually in the next three years.

Affordability. Escalating competition among broadband platforms and service providers has yielded both a proliferation of new communications and entertainment services and affordable broadband pricing for American consumers. The rapid drop in the prices for DSL broadband services in the past five years, along with the deployment of fiber infrastructure equipment, have resulted in lower prices for high-speed cable services. Despite the dramatic increase in usage, the average local monthly bill for wireless services has remained relatively stable, rising only a dime per year on average over the past four years. Satellite broadband prices have also dropped as satellite providers introduce alternative pricing models to make their services more affordable.

6

Many Americans Do Not Have Broadband Internet Access

Robert W. McChesney and John Podesta

Robert W. McChesney is the Gutgsell Endowed Professor in the department of communication at the University of Illinois at Urbana-Champaign. John Podesta is the chief executive officer and president of the Center for American Progress, a Washington, D.C., liberal public policy think tank.

While countries such as South Korea and Japan reap the economic and technological benefits of inexpensive broadband access at the highest speeds, the United States is falling behind. It is home to the most costly, slow, and unreliable high-speed Internet access in the developed world. Former President George W. Bush and the Federal Communications Commission (FCC) have stated that broadband deployment is their "highest priority." Yet their policies have stifled competition and deterred localities from establishing their own networks. In fact, major telecommunications companies, high-paid lobbyists, and their political cronies have launched a deceptive and contradictory campaign against municipal broadband, hindering the nation's economy.

Two decades ago, the chattering classes fretted about economic upheaval rising from Japan and the Asian Tigers. They feared an invasion of cars, microchips, and Karaoke that would take away American jobs, take over U.S.-dominated in-

Robert W. McChesney and John Podesta, "Let There Be Wi-Fi: Broadband Is the Electricity of the 21st Century—and Much of America Is Being Left in the Dark," *Washington Monthly*, vol. 38, January-February 2006, pp. 14–17. Copyright © 2006 by Washington Monthly Publishing, LLC, 733 15th St. NW, Suite 520, Washington, DC 20005, (202) 393-5155. www.washingtonmonthly.com. Reproduced by permission.

dustries, and shift cultural norms. In the 1990s, America responded with a boom in high technology and Hollywood exports. But a revolution is again brewing in places like Japan and South Korea. This time it's about "broadband"—a technology that, in terms of powering economies, could be the 21st century equivalent of electricity. But rather than relive the jingoism [excessive patriotism] of the 1980s, American policy makers would be wise to take a cue from the Asian innovators and implement new policies to close the digital divide at home and with the rest of the world.

Most people know broadband as an alternative to their old, slow dial-up Internet connection. These high-capacity data networks made of fiber-optic cables provide a constant, unbroken connection to the Internet. But broadband is about much more than checking your e-mail or browsing on EBay. In the near future, telephone, television, radio and the Web all will be delivered to your home via a single broadband connection. In the not-so-distant-future, broadband will be an indispensable part of economic, personal, and public life. Those countries that achieve universal broadband are going to hold significant advantages over those who don't. And so far, the United States is poised to be a follower—not a leader—in the broadband economy.

American residents and businesses now pay two to three times as much for slower and poorer quality service than countries like South Korea or Japan. Since 2001, according to the International Telecommunications Union [the United Nations agency for information and communication technology issues], the United States has fallen from fourth to 16th in the world in broadband penetration. Thomas Bleha [a journalist and former Foreign Service officer in Japan] recently argued in *Foreign Affairs* that what passes for broadband in the United States is "the slowest, most expensive and least reliable in the developed world." While about 60 percent of U.S. households do not subscribe to broadband because it is either unavailable where they live or they cannot afford it, most Japanese citizens can access a high-speed connection that's more than 10 times faster than what's available here for just $22 a month. (Japan is now rolling out ultra-high speed access at more than 500 times what the Federal Communications Commission considers to be "broadband" in this country.)

The economic ramifications are profound. "Asians will have the first crack at developing the new commercial applications, products, services, and content of the high-speed-broadband era," writes Bleha. Already, South Korea, which leads the world in the percentage of its businesses and homes with broadband, is the number one developer of online video games—perhaps the fastest-growing industry today. What's more, societies in which broadband use is near-universal will adapt to its uses much more quickly than those where access is available only to the well-to-do few.

The major obstacle to universal, affordable broadband access for all Americans is not economic or technical. It's political.

The countries surpassing the United States in broadband deployment did so by using a combination of public entities and private firms. The Japanese built their world-class system by ensuring "open access" to residential telephone lines, meaning competitors paid the same wholesale price to use the wires. The country is also establishing a super-fast, nationwide fiber system via a combination of tax breaks, debt guarantees and subsidies. But of particular note, the Japanese government also encouraged municipalities to build their own networks, especially in rural areas. Towns and villages willing to set up their own ultra-high-speed fiber networks received government subsidies covering approximately one-third of their costs.

Unfortunately, the United States has pursued the opposite policy. President [George W.] Bush has called for "universal, affordable access for broadband technology by the year 2007," and FCC [Federal Communications Commission] Chairman Kevin Martin claims broadband deployment is his "highest priority." But they have made no progress toward these goals; in fact, they have rewarded their corporate cronies for maintaining high prices, low speeds and lackluster innovation. Federal policies have not merely failed to correct our broadband problems, they have made them worse. Instead of encouraging competition, the FCC has allowed DSL [digital subscriber line] providers and cable companies to shut out competitors by denying access to their lines. And whereas the Japanese government encourages individual towns to set up their own "Community Internet," Washington [D.C.] has done nothing. Fourteen states in the United States now have laws on the books restricting cities and towns from building their own high-speed Internet networks. No wonder America is falling behind its Asian competitors.

Despite all the opposition from telecom companies and their political allies, some municipalities are finding ways to provide broadband to their residents. Community Internet projects are already up and running in dozens of small towns and coming soon to bigger cities like Philadelphia, Portland, and Minneapolis. These cities recognize broadband as perhaps the single most important factor in transforming their local economies and the lives of average citizens. Community Internet could revolutionize and democratize communications in this country. But the major obstacle to universal, affordable broadband access for all Americans is not economic or technical. It's political.

"A Birch Rod in the Cupboard"

The dispute over municipal broadband bears a striking similarity to the development of the electric power industry a century ago. As James Bailer—an attorney who represents local governments and public utilities—first warned in a 1994 pa-per written for the American Public Power Association: "The history of the electric power industry casts substantial doubt on the notion that our nation can depend on competition among cable and telephone companies alone . . . to ensure not only prompt and affordable, but also universal, access to the benefits of the information superhighway."

Borrowing from Richard Rudolph and Scott Ridley's 1986 book, *Power Struggle: The Hundred-Year War Over Electricity*, Bailer showed that when electricity first became available in the 1880s, privately owned utilities marketed "the new technology as synonymous with wealth, power and privilege," lighting large cities, businesses, and the homes of the rich. Electricity also allowed factories to stay open 24 hours a day and led to the institution of swing shifts. But communities that didn't have electricity couldn't produce as much, and couldn't keep up with urban competitors. Rural communities were left with the choice of forming a government-owned utility or being left in the dark. Even big cities like Detroit built municipal power systems to cut prices and extend service. In response, private utility companies responded with a massive propaganda and misinformation campaign that attacked advocates of municipal power as "un-American," "Bolshevik," and "an unholy alliance of radicals."

But the expansion of electricity, Bailer argued, showed that the presence—or even threat—of competition from the public sector is one of the surest ways to secure quality service and reasonable prices from private enterprises delivering critical public services. FDR [President Franklin D. Roosevelt], he notes, called municipal power systems "a birch rod in the cupboard, to be taken out and used only when the child gets beyond the point where more scolding does any good."

And Roosevelt picked up the birch rod himself. In 1935, he created the Rural Electrification Administration (REA), which gave loans and other help to small towns and farmer cooperatives interested in setting up their own power systems.

The REA turned out to be one of the New Deal's most successful programs. Within two years, hundreds of new municipal power utilities were up and running across the country, and within 20 years, virtually all of rural America had electricity, provided either by rural co-ops or big utilities spurred to action by municipal competition. Bailer concluded: "The plain, hard truth is that universal electric service would never have developed on a timely basis in the absence of municipally owned electric utilities and rural electric cooperatives"—which still account for more than a quarter of the power in the country today.

Like the advent of electricity, broadband is transforming the daily lives of Americans. The future of U.S. communities depends upon access to advanced high-speed telecommunications services, a fact many urban policymakers already recognize. "Just as with the roads of old," Dianah Neff, Philadelphia's chief information technology officer, recently told *Business-Week*, "if broadband bypasses you, you become a ghost town."

Towns in states where industry lobbyists have not succeeded (yet) in shutting down municipal broadband are doing remarkable things.

The Philadelphia Story

Last year, [in 2005] sensing their citizens were being stranded on the wrong side of the digital divide, Philadelphia's leaders launched an ambitious plan to blanket the entire city with wireless Internet service. To provide universal, affordable Internet access, Philadelphia plans to construct a gigantic "wireless mesh network"—a system of interconnected antennas placed on streetlights, traffic signals, and public buildings. Each of these "nodes" broadcasts a broadband signal, which connects up with other nodes to create a cloud of Internet access for PCs, laptops and wireless devices. The technology is similar to the "Wi-Fi hotspots" that have popped up at cafes and libraries across the country. Philadelphia's hotspot, however, will cover 135 square miles.

No tax dollars will be used to build the system, which will be financed instead with $10 to $15 million in bonds and private investment. The city is finalizing a contract with a consortium led by Earthlink to build and run the system—and several Internet service providers (ISPs) will compete to market the service to local residents. The service will cost about $20 a month—with subsidized access for lower-income households for about $10. The city plans to deploy the first of 3,000 nodes soon and complete the system by 2007.

For all its potential benefits to the city's residents, Wireless Philadelphia [the nonprofit group set up by the city to manage the project] was nearly crushed before it started. Last fall, behind closed doors in the state capitol, industry lobbyists slipped a measure into a massive telecommunications bill to stop municipalities from entering the broadband business. "The Verizon bill"—as it was known around the state legislature—sailed through both chambers before city officials and media advocates got wind of its contents. A last-minute compromise carved an exception for Philadelphia, allowing that effort to go ahead as planned, but the rest of the state was shut out.

Towns in states where industry lobbyists have not succeeded (yet) in shutting down municipal broadband are doing remarkable things. When three major employers in Scottsburg, Ind. (pop. 6,040), threatened to leave town because they didn't have the communications infrastructure needed to deal with their customers and suppliers, the town's mayor, Bill Graham, went to the major cable and telephone companies for help. They told him that extending high-speed broadband services to Scottsburg wasn't profitable enough. So the city decided to build a municipal wireless "cloud" using transmitters placed on water and electric towers that reach more than 90 percent of the surrounding county's 23,000 residents. "Scottsburg didn't wake up one morning and say, we want to be in the broadband business," Graham told PBS. "Scottsburg had business and industry that was going to leave our community because what we had was not fast enough" Scottsburg's investment worked—the employers stayed.

In Hermiston, Ore., firefighters and police officers carry wireless computers that can download blueprints of a building on the way to a fire or track an accident at the nearby Army depot that houses chemical weapons, thanks to that town's Community Internet system. And Community Internet even played a role in helping the evacuees from Hurricane Katrina. With much of the communications network obliterated in the Gulf Coast Region, a cadre of volunteers converged in Louisiana, and used donated equipment to set up wireless networks, computers and Voice over Internet Protocol (VoIP) phones at more than a dozen shelters, allowing evacuees to contact other shelters to search for family members or fill out FEMA [Federal Emergency Management Agency] forms to get disaster aid.

The Industry Backlash

Community Internet has the potential to revolutionize and democratize communications in this country. And that may be the reason why big cable and telephone companies and their political allies have launched a sophisticated misinformation campaign. These companies and their coin-operated think tanks generally make three paradoxical arguments against municipal broadband. First, they contend that municipalities have no place in the "free market." Of course, the cable and telephone giants don't mention that their own monopolies—which control 98 percent of the broadband market—have been cemented with extensive public subsidies, tax breaks and incentives (as well as free rein to tear up city streets). Verizon, for instance, didn't complain last fall when Pennsylvania handed them subsidies for broadband deployment worth nearly 10 times what Wireless Philadelphia will cost. Neither did Comcast object when Philadelphia approved a $30 million grant to build a skyscraper that will house its headquarters. To the incumbent providers, "unfair competition" means any competition at all.

Opponents also warn that municipalities will "crowd out" more efficient private players. In reality, most municipal networks are a last resort by desperate local governments. Often their choice isn't between a municipal system and a private one, but between municipal and nothing. (Of course, that doesn't stop the phone and cable companies from trying to outlaw Community Internet even in areas where they don't currently offer service.) A recent study by the Florida Municipal Electric Association found "no evidence" to support the argument that municipal systems limit private investment. On the contrary, these systems appear to spur investment by bringing entrepreneurs and new competition into the market. Even threatening to build a system has a funny way of encouraging the incumbents to improve service and lower their prices.

We need political leadership to build popular support for a new national broadband policy.

The same critics of Community Internet claim that cities are too "lazy" or inefficient to manage complex systems and will be unable to adapt to changing technologies. But municipalities have a long track record of successfully and efficiently operating power plants, sewage systems and subways. It's hard to imagine that the broadband networks—most of which will actually be operated by private contractors—are any more complex. Perhaps the more obvious question is: If these systems are destined to fail, why are the telephone and cable companies expending so much energy trying to stop them?

The high-priced industry lobbyists and their political allies are moving quickly to write their monopolies into law. In 2005, they were able to push through restrictions in five states—though only Nebraska passed an outright ban. But eight other bills were defeated or derailed thanks to a vocal coalition of media reformers, consumer groups, municipal officials, and the high-tech industry. So now opponents are pushing legislation at the federal level to outlaw municipal broadband nationwide. Rep. Pete Sessions (R-Texas), a former executive at phone giant SBC [Southern Bell Company], has introduced a bill in the House that would give incumbent providers the right of first refusal before a city or town could offer broadband service. [The bill did not become law.] A similar measure is buried in Sen. John Ensigns (R-Nev.) [2005] rewrite of the Telecom Act [Telecommunications Act of 1996].

21st Century Meal Ticket

This is exactly the opposite of what the country needs. Instead, we need political leadership to build popular support for a new national broadband policy. To start, the FCC should swiftly reverse course and restore competition for broadband whether it comes from DSL, cable, power lines, or wireless Community Internet systems.

Without real competition or innovation, broadband deployment in the United States has stagnated.

Congress could boost the speed and reliability of community wireless networks by making available more "unlicensed spectrum"—those portions of the public airwaves not exclusively reserved for government or commercial use. Existing "Wi-Fi" networks operate in "junk bands" cluttered with signals from cordless phones, microwave ovens, baby monitors and other consumer devices. At lower frequencies—like in the television band—signals travel farther and can go through walls, trees and mountains. Opening up some of this spectrum would make Community Internet systems much faster and cheaper to deploy, allowing a new generation of broadband entrepreneurs to enter the market. The broadcasters are about to return a sizable chunk of spectrum as part of the digital television transition, a portion of which could be reserved for Community Internet if Congress doesn't auction it all off to the cell phone companies. Another option would be to reallocate vast, unused "white spaces" between TV channels for wireless broadband. Either way, more "unlicensed spectrum" is the key to making universal, super-fast broadband for $10 a month a reality.

Most importantly, the federal government must ensure that the cable and telephone monopolies can't crush innovative projects like Wireless Philadelphia and the emerging national movement for Community Internet. Sens. John McCain (R-Ariz.) and Frank Lautenberg (D-N.J.) have introduced a bill [Community Broadband Act of 2005] that would free municipalities to decide for themselves which technologies best serve their citizens. U.S. policy should create incentives for communities to build advanced telecommunications networks in hundreds of cities and towns across the country, creating robust competition for communications services, assisting small entrepreneurs through public–private partnerships, and bringing opportunity to low-income urban neighborhoods and rural communities too often neglected by large entrenched monopolies.

Without real competition or innovation, broadband deployment in the United States has stagnated. And the stakes of this misguided policy couldn't be higher. According to the Department of Commerce, 95 percent of new jobs created will demand computer skills. And a 2001 Brookings Institution [a Washington, D.C., nonprofit public policy think tank] study estimated the widespread adoption of basic broadband could add $500 billion to the U.S. economy and create 1.2 million new jobs per year. Simply empowering local governments and community groups, in coordination with private entrepreneurs, to provide universal affordable, broadband may be the single best thing we can do to make America the pre-eminent economy—and democracy—of the 21st century.

7

Municipal Wireless Internet Should Be Provided

Erin Thompson

Erin Thompson graduated from Sarah Lawrence College and wrote for the Indypendent, *a New York City newspaper.*

Low-income families are much less likely to have expensive high-speed Internet access, placing them at economic and social disadvantages. To shrink this growing "digital divide," local groups across the United States are taking steps to provide broadband networks for their communities. However, powerful telecommunication companies—which have obliterated competition, charge hefty fees, and refuse to build out fiber-optic lines—lobby against such efforts in an attempt to maintain their single-payer subscription services. Still, successful municipal broadband initiatives seen from Philadelphia to San Francisco promise to democratize the Internet, and concerned citizens in other cities must also act.

On a street corner in Harlem [New York City], Kamal King and Jonathan Evans are taking pictures of light poles. They record the coordinates of each light pole and will eventually send the data to the city, which will hopefully allow them to install wireless radios on light poles around Harlem.

When installed, these radios will begin the test phases of a Harlem-wide wireless infrastructure, which the Wireless Harlem Initiative aims to use to provide free or low-cost broadband [service] to all nearby Harlem residents.

Erin Thompson, "Municipal Broadband Takes on the Internet Cartel," *Indypendent*, May 21, 2007. Reproduced by permission.

Members of NYC Wireless, a non-profit that creates wireless hotspots around the city in public parks, local businesses and low-income housing, first introduced King and Evans to the possibilities of the low-cost broadband networks at Monroe College [Bronx, New York].

"It was kind of exciting," said Evans "NYC Wireless came to our school, and this school is in the Bronx ... And these white people came to our school and were like 'hey this is wonderful.'"

For their final project in the class, King and Evans hooked up a local coffee shop with a free Wi-Fi hotspot. "We got an A," said King, who discovered the not-for-profit Wireless Harlem on the Internet one night and has been involved ever since.

Addressing the Digital Divide

On a small scale, the efforts of community groups like Wireless Harlem and NYC Wireless reflect the hundreds of initiatives undertaken by communities and municipalities around the country to address the growing "digital divide."

According to a March 2006 report by the Pew Internet and American Life Project, only 21 percent of households with an annual income of $30,000 or less had any broadband connection at home in 2006, while 68 percent of households that earn over $75,000 had a home broadband connection.

This is especially the case in Harlem, where Wireless Harlem has spent the last year doing research and advocacy to push their project forward.

"What our research told us is that there are too many people on one computer and that computer may be dial-up—and so there's a bottleneck in the household, with four or five people trying to get on one computer," said Michael Lewis, founder of Wireless Harlem. At the first of five hearings organized by the city to address the issue of Internet access, held on March 30 [2007] in the Bronx, community wireless campaigners, technology experts, policy advocates and students and teachers from the city's underserved schools testified on the conditions of broadband access in New York.

Andrew Gallagher, a public school teacher at the Bronx Writing Academy, said that only 20 percent of his students report having a computer and access to the Internet at home.

Students from New York's Brandeis High School reported that as few as nine laptops might serve 50 students, many of whom do not have Internet access at home. "Many of us even fail because we don't have computers," one student testified.

For long-time advocates of broadband access, the hearings are a first step in joining the rest of the country.

"There needs to be a wider public understanding of this issue, and that needs to be demonstrated by people showing up to these public hearings," said Laura Forlano, a board member of NYC Wireless.

Why has installing an increasingly vital communications resource—one which costs relatively little to install and maintain—become such a struggle in New York City and around the country?

Attempts to bridge the digital divide and prevent further disparities face a gauntlet of resistance from one of the most powerful industries in the country.

"The short answer is, unless someone is willing to go out and rewrite the past FCC [Federal Communications Commission] regulations and unless they open up the [telecommunications] networks to competition, there's not a rat's chance in hell that anything exciting is going to happen in New York," said Bruce Kushnick, a consumer rights' advocate and founder of Teletruth.org.

While the FCC plays an important part by setting policy, other interests play an even more profound role.

Who Really Owns the Internet?

The word "Internet" brings to mind an ever-expanding, amorphous ether of information—a network that cannot be controlled and which expands and changes as more and more people use it. Yet the Internet depends on the physical infrastructure that must support the packets of data traveling between computer networks and servers. That infrastructure includes a web of cable, telephone and fiber lines crisscrossing the United States, allowing the data to zip around the country and world.

While no one owns the Internet, a handful of powerful telephone and cable companies control the fiber, cable and copper wires that support the Internet. Competition in the telecommunications market has been obliterated by years of deregulation, mergers and the elimination of "common carrier obligations." This means attempts to bridge the digital divide and prevent further disparities face a gauntlet of resistance from one of the most powerful industries in the country.

"The main impediment to everything is the telecommunications industry—this is not even like business versus the small guy, this is a few very specific corporations versus all other business interests and human interests in the country," said Josh Breitbart, a New York-based media activist who has blogged extensively on municipal wireless initiatives.

Originally public in mission and government run (ARPANET, the forerunner of the Internet, was in part an invention of the Pentagon), a series of regulatory changes led to the gradual privatization of Internet infrastructure—with the Telecommunications Act of 1996 marking a milestone in the deregulation of the entire communications industry.

A 2005 ruling from the Supreme Court in *FCC v. Brand X Internet Services* freed the telecoms from government regulations requiring them to lease their lines at discounted rates to other Internet service providers, a concept known as common carriage requirements. This effectively gutted competition between the largest conglomerates that own most of the Internet infrastructure. Media giants like Verizon and AT&T and Time Warner, which now own most of the infrastructure, want to tack on hefty premiums for services like voice and video on top of the fees they already charge consumers for DSL [digital subscriber line], fiber and cable networks, threatening the fundamentally open nature of the Internet.

"The biggest danger for the Internet right now is that we are going to trade a binary divide of online/offline for a more subtle disparity between speed and usefulness," said Breitbart.

By doing so, the telecoms are threatening the most radical and democratic features of the Internet.

Broadband subscribers in the United States pay twice as much as customers in Asia and Europe and get a fraction of the speed.

"The Internet makes radically cheaper the provision of these once quite complicated services," said Lucas Graves, a Ph.D. candidate at Columbia University studying the history of the Internet. "If the Internet were treated as a utility, as sort of the federal highway system, and you just had a basic public trust or public investment that took care of providing the pipes, then the computers that we all use can pretty much do everything else."

Instead, telecommunications companies are set on creating a tiered toll-road for consumers, all the while squashing initiatives aimed at leveling access.

An "out-of-Control" Spiral of Divestment

While many countries around the world are investing in upgrades to fiber-to-the-home (FTTH) networks, 98 percent of Americans access the Internet via DSL and cable modem services, which, although faster than dial-up, are significantly slower than fiber optic networks. In areas deemed "economically unfeasible" for telecommunications investment, there may [be] no available alternative to dial-up. According to a January 2007 report by the Institute for Local Self-Reliance, 10 percent of U.S. households do not have access to broadband from any provider. Meanwhile, broadband subscribers in the United States pay twice as much as customers in Asia and Europe and get a fraction of the speed. First in broadband penetration rates just 10 years ago, the United States is now ranked fifteenth in the world by the Paris-based Organization for Economic Cooperation and Development.

"This is a spiral, an out-of-control spiral of us losing our competitive edge, internationally," said Sascha Meinrath, a community wireless pioneer and Internet activist.

This downward spiral is due in part to a refusal by the telecommunications industry to build out promised fiber networks. Telephone companies received $200 billion in state tax breaks and price deregulation over the past decade on the promise that they would deploy 86 million new lines of fiber infrastructure by 2006, according to Bruce Kushnick, author of *The $200 Billion Broadband Scandal.*

"The phone companies lied and took the money and didn't build the networks," Kushnick said. "And now what they're offering is basically inferior to what's currently being rolled out and deployed in Japan and other countries."

Currently, fewer than 500,000 fiber optic lines have been built. The areas where phone companies are rolling out new fiber infrastructure are almost exclusively affluent. In New York, for example, of the nearly 100 communities targeted for fiber optic deployments, 96 percent had incomes above the state median.

"In short they've hijacked the utilities to make it a private company with their own exclusive rights," Kushnick said.

Beyond the Digital Divide

At the same time that the telecommunications industry is trying to exert more and more control over the digital sphere, other forces are attempting to push the digital world in the other direction.

Some cities ... might return the Internet to its roots as an open highway that ... cannot bar some types of traffic or charge more for others.

"There are two forces that are interacting that can disrupt the current situation, one of them is technological innovation, specifically wireless, the other one is government involvement, specifically municipal," said Breitbart.

Wireless technology, which uses the same low-powered, unlicensed spectrum that garage door openers use, has been a transformative force for broadband proliferation because it allows more than one user to share an Internet connection, while being relatively cost-effective to deploy. The traditional wireless model of a "hotspot" has its limitations, however. The relatively low strength of Wi-Fi signals can only reach a few hundred feet and requires "line of sight" for access. For people in their homes, an outside signal can often be weak or nonexistent.

What's more, for anyone who doesn't own their own fiber, cable or DSL infrastructure, implementing wireless systems still means renting broadband access from an Internet service provider.

Some cities are thus pursuing options that might return the Internet to its roots as an open highway that anyone can access and which cannot bar some types of traffic or charge more for others. Successful initiatives to build municipal fiber infrastructure have been deployed across the country. One of the largest initiatives, the Utah Telecommunications Open Infrastructure Agency (UTOPIA), a publicly funded municipal broadband initiative, built fiber across 325 miles of the state and connected 250,000 homes. Many communities attempting to address the growing digital divide by implementing low-cost wireless systems or building locally owned high-speed fiber infrastructure are facing political and legal hurdles. States across the nation have rushed to pass laws prohibiting municipalities from entering the broadband market at the behest of powerful telecommunications oligopolies that funnel millions of dollars in lobbying money and campaign contribution into political coffers. When Philadelphia pursued plans to build a municipal wireless network in 2004, Verizon lobbied the state House to pass a law banning the state's municipalities from directly offering fee-based Internet service. In order to implement wireless, Philadelphia eventually signed a deal with Earthlink to build and maintain the city's wireless system, offering baseline wireless service at $22 a month and a lower-rate of $9.95 a month for low-income subscribers.

After similar displays of telecom lobbying muscle in other states, "Most other cities took a politically more palatable route," notes Forlano of NYC Wireless. By the end of 2004, 13 states had implemented laws barring municipalities from competing with incumbent broadband service providers.

While efforts like those in Philadelphia and elsewhere represent a step toward shrinking the digital divide, for community-wireless advocates they represent a missed opportunity for cities to radically restructure their Internet capabilities.

Mesh Technology

"The major providers that are doing [municipal] networks are solely doing them to maintain their single-payer model—one person pays a price for their [Internet] connection point. That's why AT&T is in this, that's why Comcast is in this—

this is why Earthlink is in this," said Meinrath, who is the co-founder of the Champaign-Urbana, Illinois Wireless Network (CUWiN).

CUWiN uses "mesh technology" to expand wireless coverage for free to anyone who has a computer and wireless card. In addition, it creates a local area network between computers using the wireless network—which can then communicate among themselves without needing an Internet connection.

While deployed on a small scale in Urbana, with only a few hundred people logged into the network on any given day, the network is a glimpse at the power that new, open-source technologies like the mesh wireless system have to connect people on a local level.

"If you have a ubiquitous wireless infrastructure that can be your communitywide broadcast station, anyone can put up a streaming server and broadcast their own radio station. Anyone can provide video . . . audio. Anyone can start doing Web hosting in their local community," said Meinrath.

Such utopian dreams—and even the possibility of building a wireless network along the lines of those in Philadelphia and San Francisco—seem far away in New York City. While most major cities already have began planning or implementing some form of a municipal broadband network in order to extend an increasingly vital resource to its citizenry, New York City has only taken the first steps in addressing broadband access.

"It's embarrassing that New York City isn't doing anything and every other major city in the U.S., if not the world, is doing something," said Bruce Lai, the chief of staff for New York City Councilwoman Gale Brewer, who chairs the City Council's Committee on Technology in Government.

Nonetheless, upcoming hearings are an opportunity for concerned citizens to pressure the city to act. "If there were just floods of people with stories that helped illustrate exactly what the problem in New York was," Forlano said, "then maybe we'd have a government solution."

"If you don't have [influence] on the side that controls most of the money and the policy," Lai concludes, "the only way to get around it is to organize."

8

Providing Municipal Wireless Internet Is Problematic

Chris Selley

Chris Selley is an assistant editor at Maclean's, *a Canadian weekly current affairs magazine.*

In 2006, municipal broadband was hailed as the failsafe way to attract businesses and help the economically disadvantaged. Yet, when several cities followed Philadelphia's lead and pursued plans to establish their own high-speed wireless networks, they were dealt crushing blows. Chicago and San Francisco, for example, were not able to agree on business terms with EarthLink. And in St. Louis and Minneapolis, technical obstacles such as power issues and weak signals dashed their communities' Wi-Fi dreams. The key lesson is that the size and business model for a broadband service must be tailored to fit the city's individual needs; municipal governments may not offer that flexibility.

Back in the heady days of pie-eyed Wi-Fi optimism—better known as 2006—there was nothing a municipal wireless Internet network couldn't do. In Chicago, it was going to attract technologically savvy businesses, make the workforce more mobile and streamline city services. In San Francisco— whose mayor, Gavin Newsom, has referred to free Wi-Fi as a "fundamental right"—it was to help lift disadvantaged neighbourhoods out of poverty. Google lent its name and its inviolable credibility to the San Francisco project in April 2006, agreeing to manage the city's free Wi-Fi while partner Earth-Link focused on a higher-speed, for-profit service. Across North America, the bells were ringing—free Wi-Fi for everyone was on the way. Cities could provide their infrastructure for free or even lease it for profit, private enterprise would bid to mount wireless access points (WAPs) all over town and people would log on in droves. Thanks to revenue from advertisements beamed into users' computers, it could all be free—or, at least, "low-cost."

Blame It on Philadelphia

It hasn't worked out, as recent weeks have dramatically illustrated. In the space of three short days in late August [2007], free Wi-Fi boosters were dealt three crushing blows. Unable to reach an agreement with either AT&T or EarthLink, each of which was demanding the city commit to purchasing bandwidth on the network, Chicago walked away from the table. A seemingly relieved EarthLink vice-president called the move "entirely appropriate," no doubt aware his embattled company was to lay off nearly half its workforce the next day. EarthLink backed out of the San Francisco deal the day after that, saying it couldn't agree to a business model "where EarthLink fronts all the money to build, own and operate the network." Members of the city's board of supervisors who had delayed ratifying the contract, some believing the network should be a purely public utility, expressed relief. But Newsom was apoplectic [furious]. "EarthLink would have been legally obligated to fulfill its promises . . . and we would have had a functioning Wi-Fi system by now," he fumed. "Now EarthLink could not be more pleased."

St. Louis figured its AT&T-designed Wi-Fi plan would make city employees more efficient—from meter maids to police officers and building inspectors—and would provide surplus bandwidth to individual citizens. When the city is a client, most industry analysts agree, the chances of success are much greater. But despite the city's less-utopian business model, its Wi-Fi dreams came undone on the same day as San Francisco's, thanks to comically low-tech circumstances. The WAPs were to be mounted on and powered by the city's street lamps, but engineers couldn't find a way to keep the juice flowing while the lights were off. "It's a major problem," a city official said.

Portland, Ore., is touted by some as a rare success story when it comes to the free, ad-based model, but there have been complaints of spotty service.

Meanwhile, Minneapolis has found the humble tree a significant obstacle. "Wi-Fi and trees don't get along very well," Joe Caldwell, CEO of USI Wireless, recently told the *Wall Street Journal*. In other cities, pre-launch boasts that Wi-Fi could draw customers away from private cable and telecom companies have run up against the simple truth that signals aren't generally strong enough to penetrate house and apartment walls without the additional expense and palaver [idle chatter] of an exterior signal booster. Even so, most networks found themselves having to install far more WAPs per city block than they had budgeted for—in some cases double the number.

EarthLink's remaining [in 2007] Wi-Fi operations—most notably in Philadelphia, New Orleans and Anaheim [Calif.]—are all subscription-based, but the company's future remains uncertain. The day after it announced the massive layoffs, it coughed up a US$5 million penalty to the city of Houston for missing a deadline to secure a lease on the city's utility poles. Portland, Ore., is touted by some as a rare success story when it comes to the free, ad-based model, but there have been complaints of spotty service. Though the provider, MetroFi, claimed a 23 per cent increase in users in July [2007] over the previous month, in many cities subscription rates have fallen far short of expectations. And MetroFi recently adjusted its business model to insist municipalities provide a guaranteed income stream—so-called "anchor tenancy" agreements. In July, having learned of this new approach, the mayor of Anchorage, [Alaska], abandoned the city's Wi-Fi plans in a huff.

How did municipalities and Internet companies get it so wrong? Blame it on Philadelphia, says wireless analyst Craig Settles, author of the 2006 book *Fighting the Good Fight for Municipal Wireless*. Or rather, blame it on the misguided hype surrounding the city's pioneering network. EarthLink agreed in October 2005 to assume all costs for managing and building out the system. Its goal, at least in part, was to gain the technical expertise necessary to bid on other cities' requests for proposals and generally position itself at the vanguard of the burgeoning "Muni Wi-Fi" movement. But it also planned to make money; the network was never intended to deliver free service supported solely by advertisements. Nevertheless, as word spread in the media and around the water cooler, "free network for Philadelphia" gradually became "free network for Philadelphians." And once Google's name was attached to the ad-driven model in San Francisco, Settles says, all nuance was lost. Nearly two years later, Settles says Philadelphia's for-profit network is still relatively on track—but the ad-driven model has been all but completely discredited.

The Key Lesson

Stephen Townsend, a veteran of urban wireless initiatives in New York and a research director at the Institute for the Future, a Silicon Valley think tank, also blames the nature of big city governments. "[It was] monorails in the '70s, convention centres in the '80s and sports stadiums in the '90s," he says, pointing to fiscally dodgy municipal fads of decades past. Jumping out in front of rival cities can be "a very easy political win" for your average mayor, Townsend notes—and lagging behind is an easy angle of attack for opponents. (Vancouver city council's motion to explore a municipal network, passed in February 2006, begins: "Whereas many cities are investing in wireless municipal infrastructure.") Keeping up with the Joneses is all very well, but if the bank forecloses on the Joneses' house and repossesses their car, you might be left looking a little silly.

Despite this, most analysts and industry leaders believe municipal governments have a key role to play in the future of such networks. Once cities calm down and conduct an "extensive needs analysis, department by department," Settles believes many will discover—as St. Louis did, before its underpowered lampposts scuttled the deal—that wireless has enormous potential to improve the efficiency of their mobile workforce and infrastructure such as parking and water meters. Companies like EarthLink and MetroFi could again be involved in building such networks, but this time they must have municipalities on board as contributing partners, rather than hype-drunk freeloaders.

If you find something that's new and innovative, the worst person to give it to is a municipal government.

The key lesson is that Wi-Fi networks need to develop more organically, to fulfill the individual needs of cities and local business. One size—and one business model—is never going to fit all, as developers in Canada have already learned. Last week [in September 2007], Toronto Hydro Telecom Inc. president David Dobbin said the OneZone network, which offers Wi-Fi over a six-square-kilometre area of downtown Toronto at a cost of $29 per month, was both profitable and exceeding subscription targets. He pointed to the company's pricing structure, its ownership of the fibre-optic network, and corporate clientele as evidence of a very different business model to the doomed Chicago and San Francisco ventures.

On the more modest end of the spectrum, the province of Saskatchewan, in partnership with provincially owned SaskTel, unveiled a free network last month covering the downtown cores of Saskatoon, Regina, Prince Albert and Moose Jaw. They claim it cost just $1.3 million from conception to launch.

In the future, however, Settles believes debate in North America will be about integrating both wired and wireless networks and public/private partnerships. Fredericton [New Brunswick] provides an early model. Its Community Network operates as a co-op, offering low-cost fibre-optic and wireless Internet to local businesses and, according to the city, spurting a period of unparalleled economic growth. Fred e-Zone, its much-vaunted free Wi-Fi network, is just a component of the overall strategy. Montreal provides yet another seemingly workable approach. Non-profit Ile Sans Fil charges businesses just $50 a year to set up and maintain a WAP—they need only cover the costs of the equipment and purchase Internet access. Accounts are free of charge for the more than 46,000 public registered users, who have their pick of nearly 140 hot spots across the island.

This flexibility was part of the glory of Wi-Fi in the first place, says Townsend, but he wasn't surprised to see big city governments flub their first kick at the can. "If you find something that's new and innovative, the worst person to give it to is a municipal government," he says. "That's where ideas go to die." For now, city-dwellers thirsting to access the Web over ubiquitous wireless broadband networks can only hope they get it right the next time around.

9

The Internet Should Be Tiered

Dena Battle

Dena Battle is vice president for policy and government affairs at the nonprofit advocacy group, the Free Enterprise Fund.

Although network neutrality legislation has been introduced that would require equal priority for all telecommunications content, Battle believes this would ultimately stifle Internet growth. Not all web content is equal, and if Internet companies were required to maintain equality, it would limit them from improving Internet connections. Ultimately, in order to keep the Internet growing and becoming faster, Battle believes that companies should be allowed to charge different prices based on the different content and bandwidth required for some Web sites.

Not all websites are equal. I know it's not politically correct to say this, and I've probably angered a thousand bloggers who used to work for the [John] Edward's [presidential] campaign. But it's true. Unfortunately, politicians in Maryland think websites should be equal—and they want a law to make it so.

Delegate Herman Taylor, who represents Montgomery County in Maryland, has introduced "net neutrality" legislation that would regulate cable and telecommunications companies by requiring equal priority for all web content. The movement behind the regulation—composed of big companies like Google and Yahoo, and bands of bloggers and activists—is hoping that with enough catchy phrases like "Don't Let the Internet Die," and "Free Internet for Everyone," it can cloud the issue, making it sound like private companies are trying to take away your MySpace page.

Instead, the movement is trying to shackle private companies from charging different prices for different services.

Not All Services Are Equal

Proponents of Internet regulation don't like to admit it, but we have net neutrality right now—it's just not mandated by the government. Cable companies are expanding and developing technology, and they've acknowledged that some of what they might be capable of doing in the future will require prioritizing services. (You may have heard of this approach before: There's a reason why HBO fans pay a little extra to get The Sopranos.) And this has folks like Google and Yahoo up in arms because they don't want to have to pay for faster service. They're happy to let consumers (you and me) do that.

Those of us who want the best and latest of all the new gizmos, like online gaming or movie downloads, might have to pay a little more for Internet service than those of us who use the web for activities that require less bandwidth.

Net neutrality isn't about your MySpace page. It's not about taking away your right to surf the Church of Twinkie website (which, incidentally, is still under construction). It's more complicated than that.

Private companies that have been spending vast amounts of dollars researching and investing to upgrade and develop new technologies don't want to keep consumers away from web content. They do, however, recognize that as the Internet grows and content and services become more varied—think videos and TV shows on demand—we might have to switch to a non-neutral net if we're to keep the web functioning. That is: Those of us who want the best and latest of all the new gizmos, like online gaming or movie downloads, might have to pay a little more for Internet service than those of us who use the web for activities that require less bandwidth.

Some Technology Requires Priority Service

One example of non-neutral technology is remote surgery. Technology is being developed that would enable a doctor to operate on a patient thousands of miles away using robotics and the Internet. Cable companies (and the patients being operated on) think this type of surgery requires prioritized bandwidth—in other words, bandwidth that is not equal with the bandwidth being used by the Planet Ketchup website.

If all Internet services had to be the same regardless of what customers paid, why would companies invest the cash to make the Internet faster?

Remote surgery is just one example of what would require priority service. We are living in an exponential era. Technological information is doubling every two years. By 2010, it's expected to double every 72 hours. Since we don't know exactly what we'll need in the future, passing net-neutral regulations now will only stifle new developments—some of which could save lives.

Moreover, the bloodlessly bureaucratic term "neutrality" falls victim to the same problems that all government price-fixing efforts face: Adam Smith's famous invisible hand [Scottish economist Adam Smith wrote that in a free market, no regulation would be needed to ensure that the mutually beneficial exchange of goods and services took place, since this "invisible hand" would guide market participants to trade in the most mutually beneficial manner]. The competing interest of all companies seeking the attention of consumers is what will ensure that the best prices fit the needs of every consumer at every level. Internet pioneers, one would think, should understand that collaborative knowledge is far superior to any single mandate handed down from the government mountaintop.

Net Neutrality Would Stifle the Internet

The bottom line is this: What keeps the Internet fast and available is competition and free-market incentives. Why do cable companies pay to upgrade technology and make service faster? So they can get more customers and make more money. If all Internet services had to be the same regardless of what customers paid, why would companies invest the cash to make the Internet faster? They wouldn't. And that's what net neutrality is asking them to do.

If you want the Internet to both grow and grow faster, leave it to the private sector. If you want to keep it equal and equally slow, bring in the government to regulate it.

10

The Internet Should Not Be Tiered

Leigh Phillips

Leigh Phillips is a European correspondent for Red Pepper, *a liberal magazine based in the United Kingdom.*

The Internet as it is now gives equal footing to large and small, from a major corporation to a lone blogger. Such egalitarianism is under threat, however. Internet service providers (ISP) seeking financial recoupment wish to turn the free Internet into a multi-tiered Internet, where "quality of service" goes to the highest bidders—big businesses and the wealthy. Champions of net neutrality are well backed, but only the largest companies could survive and compete if ISPs got their way. Also, progressives in the United States continue to raise concerns over the issue, but legislators in Europe are not impartial to the interests of telecommunications companies.

"The Internet is not something you just dump something on. It's not a big truck. It's a series of tubes."

When Republican US senator Ted Stevens made these comments last June [in 2006], he instantly became the butt of jokes across the blogosphere—not so much because he thought the Internet (or 'an' Internet, as he also put it) was a series of tubes, but because he also happens to chair the committee in charge of regulating these 'tubes'.

Worse still, the amendment under debate concerned 'net neutrality', the end of which could mean the end of the 'equal-

Leigh Phillips, "The End of the Internet?" *Red Pepper*, November 2006. Reproduced by permission.

access' Internet as we know it. The end of net neutrality would see the emergence of a two-tiered or multi-tiered Internet, with information from wealthy corporations guaranteed priority distribution to web users.

Priority Queues

In the past year, a number of the major Internet service providers in the US, including AT&T, Comcast and Verizon, have spent millions of dollars lobbying US Congress members to contest legislation that would prevent them from offering 'quality of service' guarantees to certain content providers in return for a premium fee.

Under the kind of quality of service agreements they want to offer, the ISPs [Internet service providers] would guarantee that information from premium-paying content providers reached users ahead of all other information. The websites of the large corporations (the only entities wealthy enough to afford premium fees) would load quickly and without interruption, while those of a small-time blogger might load more slowly, or not at all. This is the Internet equivalent of priority queues for business class travellers, or the guest lists that let the 'beautiful people' enter a club before the rest of us under-tanned, cellulite-stricken plebeians [lower-class citizens].

To a greater or lesser extent, the packets of information that currently wend their way across the information super-highway—not down tubes, nor on the back of a truck—are delivered blindly. There is no discrimination depending on either the type of information or where it comes from. Supporters of this status quo advocate the introduction of legislation to protect net neutrality by banning ISPs from introducing quality of service guarantee fees. But the ISPs themselves, backed by the US Chamber of Commerce, network equipment manufacturers such as Cisco Systems and neoliberal think-tanks ranging from the Cato Institute and the Ludwig von Mises Institute [libertarian think tanks] to our old friends, the

Project for a New American Century [a neoconservative think tank], argue against the introduction of any such 'restrictive' legislation.

These opponents of net neutrality claim that it is anti-competitive, inhibits innovation and presents a danger to homeland security. But their opposition to net neutrality is really born out of financial concerns. The big telecom [telecommunications] companies are attempting to recoup the costs of building improved telecommunications infrastructure from the major corporate providers of content, such as CNN and MTV, which offer bandwidth-intensive video content.

This is the Internet equivalent of . . . the guest lists that let the 'beautiful people' enter a club before the rest of us.

Quality of service guarantees are intended to sweeten this otherwise bitter pill.

The supporters of net neutrality, which include such more-or-less progressive forces as Moveon.org, the American Library Association, the American Association of Retired Persons (AARP) and the inventor of the Internet, Tim Berners-Lee, as well as several household name content providers such as Google, Yahoo and Microsoft, also deploy arguments with a 'defence-of-the-freemarket' theme. They, quite accurately, point out that a multi-tiered Internet would see discrimination in favour of existing major content providers, as upstart content providers or applications could hardly grab users' attention if access to their websites was much slower than access to those of the corporate incumbents.

The net neutrality supporters are lucky to have champions with such deep pockets, but ultimately they are looking after their own interests. Premium fees would eat into their bottom line, and so they want to avoid them. If it came to the crunch, however, and net neutrality was to wither away, the likes of

Google and Microsoft are more than wealthy enough to pay these fees and continue to survive and prosper.

The Coke boycott website, Killer Coke, . . . can be accessed as quickly as the drink's own website. This will end with the end of net neutrality.

Skewing the Market

For the rest of us, the issue is more fundamental. For all the discussion about the ever-diminishing cost of access to technology, the reality is that throughout history the means of mass communication has been at first quite widely accessible only to be later restricted. Technologies are developed that reduce the costs for larger producers while doing little to aid smaller publications, thus skewing the market towards the former.

By the first few decades of the 20th century, for example, larger newspapers had all but squeezed out the myriad small and local labour 'rags' that had earlier flourished. Today, the cost of publishing a glossy colour magazine or printing, binding and distributing an affordable paperback is similarly out of reach of virtually all but the major media conglomerates. Professional television and film production also remains, for the most part, the preserve of elite content producers, despite the development of cheap video cameras and consumer-priced video-editing software.

The Internet remains highly egalitarian by comparison. A blog by an anti-war teenager from Utah is as easy to access as the website of the US defence department. The Coke boycott website, Killer Coke, which highlights murderous labour rights abuses in Colombia associated with Coca-Cola, can be accessed as quickly as the drink's own website. This will end with the end of net neutrality.

Of course, with or without net neutrality legislation, Internet content is not immune to the myriad market conditions that favour some websites over others, ranging from search optimisation and sponsored links to plain old advertising—or simply recruiting [actors] George Clooney and John Cusack as columnists, as in the case of US liberal Ariana Huffington's overnight 'blog' success, the 'Huffington Post'. In reality, there can be no such thing as true net neutrality within the far-from-neutral market. Even so, progressives should oppose any further corporate favouritism through the appearance of quality of service guarantees. The net may not be completely neutral, but we don't want to see it become even more unequal.

In Europe, Deutsche Telekom (which owns T-Mobile in the UK [United Kingdom]) and Telecom Italia have begun to make noises similar to their American ISP counterparts.

Deutsche Telekom is in the process of constructing a fibre-optic network that will deliver information at 25 times the speed of current top-end broadband to several German cities. The cost of building this is estimated at three billion euros.

They hope to get some of that back through premium guarantees.

Not Neutral at All

Meanwhile, there is no groundswell of concern over the issue in Europe, as there is across the Atlantic. The EU [European Union] has so far taken a hands-off approach. The problem is that a neutral attitude to net neutrality—in other words, not introducing legislation to prevent telecom companies from introducing tiered pricing to content providers—is precisely the regulatory environment that the ISPs want.

The reality is that EU legislators are not neutral on the issue at all. The EU Commission is not filled with octogenarian Mr. Magoo [a nearsighted cartoon character] senators who stumble into doing what the telecommunications giants wish them to do because they think the Internet is some sort of information water slide.

Brussels [Belgium, capital of the European Union] is a haven of neoliberal fundamentalists who know precisely what the Internet is and precisely what it means to be neutral on a moving train—or truck.

11

Users Should Pay for E-Mail

Alex Gofman

Alex Gofman is vice president of Moskowitz Jacobs Inc., a marketing research and consulting firm in White Plains, New York.

Ever since the first "spam" e-mail was sent during the days of ARPANET, the Internet's predecessor, reaction has been harsh and swift. But today, from 70 to 90 percent of the 200 billion e-mails sent daily is spam. One possible, yet controversial, solution to the spam problem is a pay-per-e-mail system; at one penny a message, spam would come to a halt and billions of dollars in revenues would be generated yearly. E-mailers are also learning how to use firewalls, spam filters, and antivirus software. Laws alone may not eliminate spam, and spammers still have financial incentives to fill inboxes with suspicious solicitations.

In the funny Monty Python skit, a chorus of Vikings drowns out other sounds by singing "SPAM, SPAM, SPAM", glorifying the omnipresent American canned meat icon.

SPAM's Internet namesake is not funny at all, as it literally drowns legitimate e-mails in an outpour of junk messages.

E-mail spam, which on the insistence of the trademark owner, should be written in small letters to distinguish it from SPAM®, is surprisingly older than public e-mail: The first piece of spam was sent on May 3, 1978 (indeed, only a short time after the world's first experimental e-mail message was sent in 1971 by Ray Tomlinson). The first spam was addressed

Alex Gofman, "Pay per E-mail System Would Sound the Death Knell for Spam," *DNA*, February 21, 2009. Reproduced by permission.

to a list taken from a printed directory of ARPANET users—the first major wide-area computer network. At that time, it was comprised mostly of universities and select corporations, making the subject of the spam especially apt—a new computer system.

The reaction to this act of aggressive marketing was swift. One MIT professor angrily suggested nobody should be allowed to send messages with headers that long, no matter the subject, although he complained about that as well. The first spam quickly gave birth to the first spam fighters. The US military, which controlled ARPANET, issued a stern warning to every user on the network. Since then, much has changed. The original small group of privileged users exchanging a few occasional short messages grew to 1.3 billion e-mail users worldwide sending more than 200 billion e-mails every day (over 2 million every second.)

By some estimates, between 70–90% of this volume is spam. If every spam sent in a single day were a can of SPAM®, there would easily be enough to feed all the hungry of the world for a year. This suggests a possible (although highly controversial) solution to the spam problem—charging a small fee for every e-mail sent out—even if only a penny. For sure it would eliminate almost all spam, but what about the legitimate users of e-mail? Are we ready to pay a few extra dollars for a spam-free world? Apparently, most netizens [citizens of the Internet] are not keen to the idea. Too bad. A single penny per e-mail could go a long way towards not only exterminating pest spam, but also helping to solve major global problems. With a penny "per" toll with the current volume of e-mails, the revenues would cover the initial US economic bailout cost of $700 billion in just a year. But my calculator is itching to share more fun facts: If you were to put all the pennies from a year's worth of e-mails side by side, the chain would reach the Sun 10 times! Our Moon is too easy a target—it would take only several hours to build a spine of pennies for the new space elevator.

Not So Bleak

In November 2008, the FBI [U.S. Federal Bureau of Investigation] scored a major victory by shutting down what they deemed the main spam portal. The US-based company, McColo Corp, catered to bulk e-mailers, and its deactivation cut the amount of global spam more than in half in just one day. The relief did not last, unfortunately—in just a few days the perpetrators, very much like Hydra [mythological many-headed serpent], regenerated their amputated limbs and were back in business with a vengeance, running it from other countries.

The future, however, is not so bleak. Education is beginning to take effect. Many home users are now protected by firewalls, antivirus software and spam filters. Through enforceable Internet policies, businesses prevent employees from sending spam. Even Microsoft is engaged in the battlefield and future versions of Windows might be 'bullet-proof' to spam.

According to MSNBC, Internet provider Earthlink, which has approximately 5 million subscribers, boasts its "Spam-Blocker" can eliminate spam "virtually 100%." The system uses the "challenge-response" technique that requests proof of identity from unknown senders.

With a penny "per" toll with the current volume of e-mails, the revenues would cover the initial US economic bailout cost of $700 billion in just a year.

Spam-protection strategies range from small to legal to geo-political. Unfortunately, neither method is universal. If a spam filter tries to block the word 'cialis', it also removes all legitimate e-mails containing the word 'specialist'. In the US, there are several existing and proposed legislations that are intended to fight spam, among them requiring marketers to allow people to easily remove their e-mail addresses from bulk lists, and banning non-existing return e-mail addresses. There's also a movement to set up a "no-spam" registry similar to the Federal Trade Commission's do-not-call list for telemarketers. On a global scale, some suggest such radical measures as 'cutting' entire countries harboring spammers off the net. This is not likely to happen any time soon though, as the biggest source of spam is the US.

Even legal experts do not expect the laws alone to wipe out spam, although tough criminal and civil penalties could be a strong deterrent. Spammers make their living while there is a receptive audience for cheap Rolexes, offers to raise the manhood ego, solicitations to redeem an inheritance from Nigeria and a chance to make a quick buck exploiting commercial market research surveys. The most efficient method for spam extermination is simple and low-tech: Just don't open spam. If spammers do not have business, there is no reason to send more offers. If we do not use them, they will be out of cash and out of business soon.

12

Users Should Not Pay for E-Mail

Wendy M. Grossman

Wendy M. Grossman is a technology writer and contributor to Reason *magazine.*

In order to prevent junk e-mail from overtaking consumers' in-boxes, some companies have proposed a pay-per-e-mail system. The system requires the sender to pay a price per e-mail they send out, in hopes of preventing, or limiting, junk e-mail. Allowing a system that requires a user to pay for e-mail would have negative effects, and essentially kill free service providers such as Hotmail and Yahoo.

From time to time, someone proposes an economic solution to spam. There are a number of variations, but they all boil down to one idea: You should pay, literally, for all the e-mails you send. This is a popular idea because even a tiny charge that wouldn't cost individual users very much would impose a substantial burden on spammers. At a penny per e-mail, for instance, sending 1 million messages would cost $10,000. At the very least, such a fee would get spammers to clean their lists.

The Problems of Paying for E-mail

There are several problems with this idea. First and foremost, no ISP in the world is set up to charge this way. It would require an entirely new infrastructure for the industry. In addition, charging for e-mail would kill free services such as Yahoo! and Hotmail in a single stroke and, with greater social costs, make today's many valuable mailing lists economically unfeasible.

If we had micropayments—that is, the technical ability to manage transactions of a penny or even fractions of a penny— we'd have more flexibility to consider charging schemes with fewer social costs. If, for example, you could require that unknown correspondents attach one cent to an e-mail message, you could void the payment for wanted e-mail, leaving only the spammers to pay it.

But we don't have micropayments and we have little immediate prospect of getting them. Given the costs to the industry of altering its billing infrastructure, the only way a pay-per-message scheme would work is if it were legally mandated—and even then, such a mandate could not be imposed worldwide.

Charging for e-mail would kill free services such as Yahoo! and Hotmail in a single stroke.

In one of the biggest turnarounds in Net history, many people who formerly opposed the slightest hint of government regulation online are demanding anti-spam legislation. So far, the European Union has made spam illegal, 34 states in the U.S. have banned it, and a number of competing federal bills are in front of Congress, which has considered such legislation before. Various proposed federal laws would require spam to include labels, opt-out instructions, and physical addresses; to ban false headers; to establish a do-not-mail registry; or to ban all unsolicited advertising. Most of the state laws require labeling and opt-out mechanisms.

An Opt-out System Would Be More Effective

Not everyone is happy with the U.S. legislation's provisions, however: Steve Linford, head of Europe's Spamhaus Project, says America's opt-out approach will legalize flooding the world with spam. He notes that the world's 200 biggest spammers are all based in Florida. With an opt-out system, anyone would have the right to put you on any list at any time, as long as they remove you if you request it. Linford believes instead that "opt in"—prohibiting companies from adding addresses to lists unless their owners have given their specific consent—is the key to effective anti-spam legislation.

Whatever the merits of Linford's and others' proposals, there's an important point to remember: None of the anti-spam laws passed so far has been effective, and that's not likely to change. Lots of spam includes opt-out instructions that don't work; the key is getting businesses to honor them. A do-not-mail registry would double as a free address registry for spammers based offshore. And requiring a physical address for the sender would, like any mandated identification system, make anonymous speech on the Net illegal. Just about everyone is against spam, but most people are for anonymous speech and its ability to let whistleblowers and other vulnerable people speak their minds. Existing and proposed legislation seriously threatens anonymity, raising legitimate worries about censorship.

The ultimate problem with legislation is that spam is a global problem, not a state or federal one. A patchwork of conflicting laws will do nothing to improve the ease of use of e-mail communications. None of the laws so far passed have diminished the amount of spam flooding the Net. Lawrence Lessig, a Stanford law professor and the author of *Code and Other Laws of Cyberspace*, believes the problem is enforcement, and his proposal is for the government to pay a bounty to any geek who can track down and identify a spammer. He's even offered to quit his job if this scheme is tried for a year and fails.

The Usenet Experience

There's one more approach to the spam problem that we should consider. For the lack of a better term, we might call it the community solution. Alternatively, we could call it the Usenet approach.

Created in 1979, Usenet is in many respects still the town square of the Internet. It played that role even more in 1994, when the Web was still in its "before" stage and two Arizona lawyers, Martha Siegel and Laurence Canter, sent out an infamous spam advertising their services, provoking a furious reaction. The technical method used to post the message meant that you couldn't mark it read in one newsgroup and then not see it in the others, so anyone reading a number of Usenet newsgroups saw the message in every single group.

When the uproar eventually settled, a new hierarchy of ad-friendly newsgroups was created, each beginning with the prefix "biz." But this approach never really worked, because the kind of people who advertise anti-cellulite cream, get-rich-quick schemes, and cable descramblers don't care if they annoy people; they just want maximum eyeballs. In the ad hoc newsgroup news.admin.net-abuse.usenet, users and administrators discussed and developed a system that took advantage of the cancellation features built into Usenet's design. These are primarily designed so people can cancel their own messages, but a number of public-spirited people hacked them so third parties could use them to cancel spam.

By now spam has died out in many newsgroups, partly because the system worked and partly because the spammers simply moved to e-mail's wider audience. But the worst spam period cost Usenet many of its most valuable and experienced posters, who retreated to e-mail lists and more private forms of communication and have never come back.

The key to making this system work was community standards that defined abuse in terms of behavior rather than content. Spam was defined as substantively identical messages, posted to many newsgroups (using a threshold calculated with a mathematical formula) within a specified length of time. The content of the message was irrelevant. These criteria are still regularly posted and can be revised in response to community discussion. Individual communities (such as newsgroups run by companies or ISPs) can set their own standards. It is easy for any site that believes canceling spam threatens free speech to block the cancels and send an unfiltered newsfeed.

If everyone with the technical capability to run a server offered five friends free, filtered e-mail, many consumers would be able to reclaim their inboxes.

The issues raised by Usenet spam were identical to those raised by junk e-mail today. The community, albeit a much smaller one, managed to create standards supported by consensus, and it came up with a technical scheme subject to peer review. A process like this might be the best solution to the spam e-mail problem. The question is whether it's possible given the much more destructive techniques spammers now use and given the broader nature of the community.

Free, Filtered E-mail Would Help Stop Spam

Some working schemes for blocking spam are based on community efforts—in which the first recipients of a particular spam send it in, for example, so it can be blocked for other users in the group. In addition, the Net has a long tradition of creating tools for one's own needs and distributing them widely so they can be used and improved for the benefit of all. As in the Usenet experience, there is very little disagreement on what spam is; that ought to make it easier to develop good tools. I can't create those tools, but I can offer less technical friends a spam-filtered e-mail address on my server, which has SpamAssassin integrated into it (after a month of work to get it running), to help them get away from the choked byways of Hotmail or AOL. If everyone with the technical capability to run a server offered five friends free, filtered e-mail, many consumers would be able to reclaim their inboxes. Some ISPs are beginning to offer—and charge for—such a service.

In the end, the ISPs are crucial to this fight. In the Usenet days, system administrators would sometimes impose the ultimate sanction, the Usenet Death Penalty—a temporary block on all postings from an ISP that had been deaf to all requests to block spam sent from its servers. It usually took only a couple of days for the offending ISP to put better policing in place—the customers would demand it. That's what the Real-time Blackhole Lists do, constructing their databases of known spam sources from pooled reports. But the bigger and richer ISPs, such as Hotmail and AOL, can take the lead by taking legal action, as they are beginning to do. AOL filed five anti-spam lawsuits last spring alone.

The Usenet experience shows that the Net can pull together to solve its own problems. I don't think we're anywhere near the limits of human technical ingenuity to come up with new and more effective ways of combating spam, any more than I think e-mail is the last electronic medium that spammers will use. (There have been a couple of cases of "blogspam," where robot scripts have posted unwanted advertising to people's blogs.) The problem of spam may be a technical arms race, but it's one that's likely to be much easier to win than a legislative arms race.

When I spoke with Danny Meadowes-Klue, head of the U.K.'s [United Kingdom's] Interactive Advertising Bureau, he told me, "Spam is the biggest threat to the Internet." But he didn't mean what you think he meant. He was talking about the destructiveness of so many efforts to stop it.

13

Minorities Are Closing the Digital Divide

Michel Marriott

Michel Marriott is a staff writer for the New York Times, *specializing in education and consumer technology.*

Compared with more than a decade ago, blacks, Hispanics, and other groups in the United States are gaining Internet access at a steady pace. The increased affordability of laptops and other devices, more computers in public libraries and schools, and evolving Internet culture have dramatically narrowed the ethnic technology gap. Observing these positive trends, experts and policymakers had been worried for years that the Web and its technologies were bypassing blacks and other minorities in contrast to whites and Asians. Nonetheless, some challenges lie ahead. Commentators disagree on whether many black and Hispanic youths use the Internet for civic or business activities and advanced projects, and users who depend on institutions for Internet usage have limited options.

African-Americans are steadily gaining access to and ease with the Internet, signaling a remarkable closing of the "digital divide" that many experts had worried would be a crippling disadvantage in achieving success.

Civil rights leaders, educators and national policy makers warned for years that the Internet was bypassing blacks and some Hispanics as whites and Asian-Americans were rapidly increasing their use of it.

Michel Marriott, "Digital Divide Closing as Blacks Turn to Internet," *New York Times*, March 31, 2006. Reproduced by permission.

But the falling price of laptops, more computers in public schools and libraries and the newest generation of cell phones and hand-held devices that connect to the Internet have all contributed to closing the divide, Internet experts say.

Another powerful influence in attracting blacks and other minorities to the Internet has been the explosive evolution of the Internet itself, once mostly a tool used by researchers, which has become a cultural crossroad of work, play and social interaction.

Studies and mounting anecdotal evidence now suggest that blacks, even some of those at the lower end of the economic scale, are making significant gains. As a result, organizations that serve African-Americans, as well as companies seeking their business, are increasingly turning to the Internet to reach out to them.

Blacks and other members of minorities of various ages are . . . merging onto the digital information highway as never before.

"What Digital Divide?"

"What digital divide?" Magic Johnson, the basketball legend, asked rhetorically in an interview about his new Internet campaign deal with the Ford Motor Company's Lincoln Mercury division to use the Internet to promote cars to black prospective buyers.

The sharpest growth in Internet access and use is among young people. But blacks and other members of minorities of various ages are also merging onto the digital information highway as never before.

According to a Pew national survey of people 18 and older, completed in February [2006], 74 percent of whites go online, 61 percent of African-Americans do and 80 percent of English-speaking Hispanic-Americans report using the Internet. The survey did not look at non-English-speaking Hispanics, who some experts believe are not gaining access to the Internet in large numbers.

In a similar Pew survey in 1998, just 42 percent of white American adults said they used the Internet while only 23 percent of African-American adults did so. Forty percent of English-speaking Hispanic-Americans said they used the Internet.

Despite the dissolving gap, some groups like the Intel Computer Clubhouse Network, which introduces digital technologies to young people, say the digital divide is still vast in more subtle ways. Instant messaging and downloading music is one thing, said Marlon Orozco, program manager at the network's Boston clubhouse, but he would like to see black and Hispanic teenagers use the Internet in more challenging ways, like building virtual communities or promoting their businesses.

Vicky Rideout, vice president of the Henry J. Kaiser Family Foundation, which has studied Internet use by race, ethnicity and age, cautioned that a new dimension of the digital divide might be opening because groups that were newer to the Internet tended to use less-advanced hardware and had slower connection speeds.

"The type and meaningful quality of access is, in some ways, a more challenging divide that remains," Ms. Rideout said. "This has an impact on things like homework."

In addition, Internet access solely at institutions can put students at a disadvantage. Schools and other institutions seldom operate round the clock, seven days a week, which is especially an issue for students, said Andy Carvin, coordinator for the Digital Divide Network, an international group that seeks to close the gap.

The Internet Is More than a Luxury

But not everyone agrees that minorities tend toward less-advanced use of the Internet. Pippa Norris, a lecturer on comparative politics at Harvard who has written extensively about the digital divide, said members of minorities had been shown to use the Internet to search for jobs and to connect to a wide variety of educational opportunities.

"The simple assumption that the Internet is a luxury is being disputed by this group," Ms. Norris said.

The divide was considered so dire a decade ago that scholars, philanthropists and even President Bill Clinton in his 1996 State of the Union address fretted over just what the gap would mean in lost educational and employment opportunities for young people who were not wired.

In an effort to help erase the divide, the federal government has provided low-cost connections for schools, libraries, hospitals and health clinics, allocated money to expand in-home access to computers and the Internet for low-income families and given tax incentives to companies donating computer and technical training and for sponsoring community learning centers.

As a result of such efforts, "most kids, almost all kids, have a place in which they can go online and have gone online," said Ms. Rideout of the Kaiser foundation.

Jason Jordan of Boston is one of the young people closing the divide. Jason, 17, who is black, is getting a used computer from an older brother. He said he had wanted a computer for years, since "I heard about a lot that I was missing."

Jason said he had access to the Internet at school, where he is pursuing a general equivalency diploma, but looked forward to having his own computer and Web access at his home in the Dorchester section of Boston. "I can work in my own place and don't have to worry about the time I'm online," he said.

Like Jason, almost 9 out of 10 of the 21 million Americans ages 12 to 17 use the Internet, according to a report issued in July by the Pew Internet and American Life Project. Of them, 87 percent of white teenagers say they use the Internet, while 77 percent of black teenagers and 89 percent of Hispanic teenagers say they have access to it, the report said.

The gap in access among young Americans is less pronounced than among their parents' generation, said Susannah Fox, associate director of the Pew project. "Age continues to be a strong predictor for Internet use," Ms. Fox said.

While overall Internet use among blacks still significantly trails use among whites, the shrinking divide is most vividly reflected in the online experience of people like Billy and Barbara Johnson. Less than two years ago, the Johnsons, who are black, plugged into the Internet in their upscale suburban home near Atlanta for the first time. Mrs. Johnson, a 52-year-old mother of four and homemaker, said she felt she had little choice because her school-age children needed to use the Internet for research.

And then there is e-mail. "No one really wants to take the time anymore to pick up the phone and keep in touch," lamented Mrs. Johnson, who said that so much of the communications with her children's school was done through e-mail correspondence. "I felt like I was pretty much forced into it."

Even so, Mrs. Johnson said her husband, an assistant coach for the Atlanta Falcons, still chided her when she neglected to check her e-mail at least every day.

Progress on the Horizon

Ms. Norris and other experts on Internet use see progress on the horizon. They note that the declining cost of laptop and other computers, and efforts, like those in Philadelphia, to provide low-cost wireless Internet access, are likely to increase online access for groups that have been slow to connect.

Philanthropic efforts have also helped to give more people Internet access. For example, the Bill and Melinda Gates Foundation has awarded $250 million since 1997 for American public libraries to create Internet access for the public. Martha Choe, the foundation's director of global libraries, said some 47,000 computers had been bought for 11,000 libraries. Today, Ms. Choe said, most libraries in the United States have public Internet access.

With so many more members of minorities online, some
Web sites are trying to capitalize on their new access.

Education levels remain a major indicator of who is among the 137 million Americans using the Internet and who is not, said Ms. Fox.

There is also a strong correlation, experts say, between household income and Internet access.

With so many more members of minorities online, some Web sites are trying to capitalize on their new access. For example, the New York/New Jersey region of the State of the African American Male, a national initiative to improve conditions for black men, is encouraging men to use digital equipment to "empower themselves" to better their lives. The site, which includes studies, public policy reports and other information about issues related to black men, promotes using digital cameras, mobile phones and iPods, but mainly computers, to organize through the Internet, said Walter Fields, vice president for government relations for the Community Service Society, an antipoverty organization, and a coordinator of the black-male initiative. Users are encouraged to submit articles, write blogs and upload pertinent photographs and video clips.

"What we're doing is playing against the popular notion of a digital divide," Mr. Fields said. "I always felt that it was a misnomer."

14

The Digital Divide Is Still a Problem

Brian L. Hawkins and Diana G. Oblinger

Brian L. Hawkins is president and Diana G. Oblinger is vice president of EDUCAUSE, a nonprofit association that focuses on higher education and information technology.

Recent statistics for computer ownership and Internet usage are, indeed, encouraging. Nonetheless, the digital divide has a second level for students, which may be related to the computer's condition, connectivity (e.g., dial-up, broadband), online skills, autonomy and freedom of access, and technology support. For instance, having an old computer with insufficient memory and outdated software is a disadvantage. Broadband access is also not as accessible in rural areas or to low-income households, and not all students are digitally literate or have consistent support from help desks and peers. Thus, computer ownership and the wiring of communities do not guarantee equal Internet access.

Who can get through a day without going online? We shop online, bank online, and browse a broad array of information online. Students network through sites like Facebook.com or MySpace. Technology is nearly ubiquitous on campus. Every K-12 school in the United States is connected to the Internet. And there is a computer in every home, right? Well, no, not really. Although conversations about the digital divide are now relatively uncommon, it would be incorrect to assume that all students own a computer or have an Internet connection.

Brian L. Hawkins and Diana G. Oblinger, "The Myth About the Digital Divide," *EDUCAUSE Review*, July/August 2006, pp. 12–13. Reproduced by permission.

Many computer-ownership figures are encouraging. For example, the median for computer ownership by students at all campuses participating in the 2004 EDUCAUSE Core Data Survey was 80 percent. This figure could be interpreted to mean that the digital divide is almost gone. But even though the median was 80 percent, the statistical average was 67 percent—indicating that there are differences among campuses. At private colleges and universities, computer ownership averaged 81 percent; at public institutions, the figure was 59 percent. And those numbers still don't tell the entire story. At private doctoral institutions, 91 percent of all students owned their own computer; at public two-year institutions (community colleges and junior colleges), the figure was 35 percent.

Although computer ownership is not 100 percent, progress has been made on closing the digital divide. Student computer ownership grew from 51 percent in 2002 to 67 percent in 2004. And increases were found across all categories of institutions. For example, computer ownership at community colleges jumped from 12 percent to 34 percent during that two-year period. Even so, public computing labs are still needed. Not all students own computers. Some students own computers that do not have the processing power or software required for their courses. Others students lack, or cannot afford, broadband access where they live. Public computing labs are also convenient. Students who own laptops often prefer to use a lab while on campus rather than carrying a machine all day.

The Second-Level Digital Divide

Defining the digital divide according to the haves and have-nots of computer ownership is only a starting point. Beyond computer ownership, colleges and universities should explore the second-level digital divide, which can be caused by several factors: machine vintage; connectivity; online skills; autonomy and freedom of access; and computer-use support. The definition of *digital divide* must include all of these other factors.

Possessing current technology, with sufficient memory and speed, is critical for technical access. The capabilities of a new computer contrast starkly with those of a five-year-old refurbished machine. Although a refurbished older machine may be helpful, it can pose some significant limitations. Refurbished machines are often provided with no operating system or applications because of licensing issues. Can the student afford to purchase the operating system? The applications? Will current versions of software even run on an older machine?

Public computing labs are still needed.

Connectivity can be an issue as well. Access to broadband, rather than dial-up, influences how often, how long, and how effectively the Internet is used. As broadband access increases, so does time spent online and user satisfaction. Yet it would be incorrect to assume that broadband is universally available—or affordable. At the end of 2005, only 24 percent of rural Americans had broadband access, compared with 39 percent of urban and suburban dwellers. With many colleges and universities located in non-urban areas, and with most students living off-campus, broadband may not be affordable, or even accessible, to all students.

Differences in online skills—the ability to efficiently and effectively find information on the Web—constitute another factor in the digital divide. Not all students arrive at college digitally literate. This may be due to lack of technology access or training prior to college. Although current K-12 students have a mandated technology exposure, the same may not be true for adult learners. Most will have graduated from high school before the current computer requirements; some will have been in workplaces where technology was not used. For those with lower levels of technology skill, tasks take longer to complete and are more often abandoned. As [sociology professor] Eszter Hargittai has noted, if users often give up in frustration and confusion, then merely having access does not mean that a digital divide has been solved because a divide remains in their capacity to effectively use the Internet.

Autonomy and freedom of access represent another factor. Students who have a well-configured computer and broadband where they live have 24x7 access to information. However, students who share a computer or who must go to a public lab are limited by when a facility is open, when a computer is available, when they can get transportation to campus, and so on. The use of a shared machine is much lower than the use of a personal machine.

Even in the increasingly electronic world of classes and campus activities, neither individual access nor digital literacy should be assumed.

Finally, virtually everyone has questions about technology use, with issues spanning technology, content, disciplinary knowledge, and instructional expectations. Without readily available support, these questions can contribute to a second-level digital divide. Even if support is available, is it from someone who is skilled, both in the technology and in how to help a novice user? Students often turn to each other for help with technology, but it would be incorrect to assume that student experts or effective helpdesks are always available. Both lack of support and poor-quality support can dampen confidence and use. As Hargittai has noted: Policy decisions that aim to reduce inequalities in access to and use of information technologies must take into consideration the necessary investment in training and support as well. Like education in general, it is not enough to give people a book; we also have to teach them how to read in order to make it useful. Similarly, it is not enough to wire all communities and declare that everyone now has equal access to the Internet. People may have technical access, but they may still continue to lack effective access in that they may not know how to extract information for their needs from the Web.

Strategic Questions

In thinking about the digital divide, college and university leaders should ask themselves the following strategic questions:

1. *Do we know whether students have a computer? Do we know their skill level?* Although it is easy to assume that all students own a computer and are computer-literate, is that a correct description of the student body? Is ownership the same for all students, or are there significant differences between groups, such as traditional-age students and adult learners? Are there different needs based on academic discipline?

2. *Do we look beyond who has Internet access to consider online skills?* What online skills, support, and freedom of use define an appropriate threshold for digital access and use on campus?

3. *Do we limit the definition of digital divide to a haves and have-nots dichotomy?* The digital divide is not a yes-no proposition; it is a continuum. Beyond computer ownership lie issues of Internet access at a reasonable speed, as well as availability of support. The campus may need to define its own metrics to determine the extent of its underserved, digital divide population.

4. *How limiting will inadequate online skills be to students?* The ultimate issue behind the digital divide is the ability of students to learn, explore, and become participating members of their chosen communities. Education is increasingly dependent on students technical proficiency not only to find information but also to analyze material and access experts. If students are regularly expected

to participate in online discussions or use tools such as wikis [sites that can be collaboratively edited], campuses should provide reasonable support to ensure that students can participate effectively and autonomously.

Both the first- and the second-level digital divides should continue to be a concern for academic, student life, and IT [information technology] professionals and leaders on campus. Even in the increasingly electronic world of classes and campus activities, neither individual access nor digital literacy should be assumed. There is still a digital divide.

Organizations to Contact

The editors have compiled the following list of organizations concerned with the issues debated in this book. The descriptions are derived from materials provided by the organizations. All have publications or information available for interested readers. The list was compiled on the date of publication of the present volume; the information provided here may change. Be aware that many organizations take several weeks or longer to respond to inquiries, so allow as much time as possible.

Berkman Center for Internet & Society
Harvard University, 23 Everett St., 2nd Fl.
Cambridge, MA   02138
(617) 495-7547 • fax: (617) 495-7641
e-mail: cyber@law.harvard.edu
Web site: http://cyber.law.harvard.edu

The Berkman Center was founded to explore cyberspace, share in its study, and help pioneer its development. The center represents a network of faculty, students, fellows, entrepreneurs, lawyers, and virtual architects working to identify and engage with the challenges and opportunities of cyberspace. Its faculty, fellows, students, and affiliates engage with a wide spectrum of Internet issues, including governance, privacy, intellectual property, antitrust, content control, and electronic commerce.

Cato Institute
1000 Massachusetts Ave. NW, Washington, DC   20001-5403
(202) 842-0200 • fax: (202) 842-3490
Web site: www.cato.org

Founded in 1977, the mission of the Cato Institute is to increase the understanding of public policies based on the principles of limited government, free markets, individual liberty, and peace. The institute aims to use the most effective means to originate, advocate, promote, and disseminate applicable policy proposals that create free, open, and civil societies in the United States and throughout the world. The Cato Institute opposes municipal broadband.

Center for Digital Media Freedom (CDMF)
1444 I St. NW, Suite 500, Washington, DC   20005
(202) 289-8928 • fax: (202) 289-6079
e-mail: mail@pff.org
Web site: www.pff.org

Maintained by the Progress & Freedom Foundation, the CDMF promotes liberal public policy regarding all forms of communications, as well the freedom of speech and expression. Its goal is maximizing media freedom both in a structural (business) sense and a social (speech-related) sense.

Electronic Frontier Foundation (EFF)
454 Shotwell St., San Francisco, CA   94110-1914
(415) 436 9333 • fax: (415) 436 9993
e-mail: eff@eff.org
Web site: www.eff.org

EFF is an organization of students and other individuals that aims to promote a better understanding of telecommunications issues. It fosters awareness of civil liberties issues arising from advancements in computer-based communications media and supports litigation to preserve, protect, and extend First Amendment rights in computing and telecommunications technologies. EFF's publications include the electronic newsletter *EFFector Online* and online bulletins and publications.

Internet Society (ISOC)
1775 Wiehle Ave., Suite 102, Reston, VA   20190-5108
(703) 326-9880 • fax: (703) 326-9881
e-mail: isoc@isoc.org
Web site: www.isoc.org

A group of technologists, developers, educators, researchers, government representatives, and businesspeople, ISOC supports the development and dissemination of standards for the Internet and works to ensure global cooperation and coordination for the Internet and related Internet-working technologies and applications. It publishes the bimonthly magazine *On the Internet*.

National Telecommunications and Information Administration (NTIA)

Herbert C. Hoover Building
U.S. Department of Commerce/NTIA
1401 Constitution Ave. NW, Washington, DC   20230
(202) 482-2000
Web site: www.ntia.doc.gov

NTIA is an agency within the U.S. Department of Commerce that serves as the executive-branch agency principally responsible for advising the president on telecommunications and information policies. In this role, the NTIA frequently works with other executive-branch agencies to develop and present the administration's position on these issues. Its offices include the Institute for Telecommunication Sciences and the Office of Telecommunications and Information Applications.

New America Foundation

1899 L St. NW, Suite 400, Washington, DC   20036
Web site: www.newamerica.net

The New America Foundation is a nonprofit, nonpartisan public policy institute that invests in new thinkers and new ideas to address the next generation of challenges facing the United States. The foundation's mission is animated by the American ideal that each generation will live better than the last. New America supports municipal broadband and publishes articles and policy papers on the Internet.

SavetheInternet.com Coalition

Web site: www.savetheinternet.com

A project of the Washington, D.C.-based Free Press, Savethe Internet.com is a coalition of more than a million members and thousands of nonprofit organizations, businesses, and bloggers working to protect Internet freedom. It upholds that the Internet is a crucial engine for economic growth, civic engagement, and free speech. It works in favor of net neutrality, which the coalition claims will ensure that the Internet remains open to new ideas, innovation, and voices.

Bibliography

Books

Robert Bell et al., eds. — *Broadband Economies: Creating the Community of the 21st Century*. New York: Intelligent Community Forum, 2008.

Robert J. Deibert et al., eds. — *Access Denied: The Practice and Policy of Global Internet Filtering*. Cambridge, MA: MIT Press, 2008.

Martin Fransman — *Global Broadband Battles: Why the U.S. and Europe Lag While Asia Leads*. Stanford, CA: Stanford Business Books, 2006.

Jack Goldsmith and Tim Wu — *Who Controls the Internet?: Illusions of a Borderless World*. New York: Oxford University Press, 2006.

Thomas M. Leonard and Randolph J. May, eds. — *Net Neutrality or Net Neutering: Should Broadband Internet Services Be Regulated?* New York: Springer, 2006.

Jonathan E. Nuechterlein and Philip J. Weiser — *Digital Crossroads: American Telecommunications Policy in the Internet Age*. Cambridge, MA: MIT Press, 2005.

Dawn C. Nunziato — *Virtual Freedom: Net Neutrality and Free Speech in the Internet Age*. Stanford, CA: Stanford Law Books, 2009.

Scott A. Snyder	*The New World of Wireless: How to Compete in the 4G Revolution.* Upper Saddle River, NJ: Wharton School Publishing, 2010.
Don Tapscott and Anthony D. Williams	*Wikinomics: How Mass Collaboration Changes Everything.* New York: Portfolio, 2008.
Jonathan L. Zittrain	*The Future of the Internet—And How to Stop It.* New Haven, CT: Yale University Press, 2009.

Periodicals

Martin H. Bosworth	"Municipal Wi-Fi: The Internet's Next Step?" www.ConsumerAffairs.com, August 17, 2006.
Andy Carvin	"The Gap," *School Library Journal*, March 2006.
Shawn Chang	"The High Stakes of Net Neutrality," *Rural Telecommunications*, January–February 2009.
Jeff Chester	"The End of the Internet?" *Nation*, February 1, 2006.
Esther Dyson	"You've Got Goodmail," *New York Times*, March 17, 2006.
Kevin Fitchard	"Broadband for All," *Telephony*, September 15, 2008.

Carole E. Handler	"The Struggle over Net Neutrality," *e-Commerce Law & Strategy*, February 1, 2009.
David Haskin	"Get Ready for the Next Wave of Wireless" *Computerworld*, May 14, 2007.
Elaine C. Kamarck	"Increasing Internet Capacity," *Boston Globe*, December 26, 2007.
Steven Levy	"True or False: U.S.'s Broadband Penetration Is Lower Than Even Estonia's," *Newsweek*, July 2, 2007.
PC Magazine Online	"Is Municipal Wi-Fi a Right? If So, Who Pays?" June 21, 2006.
Karsten Polke-Majewski	"Too Big To Control?" *Atlantic Times*, June 2008.
Andrew Sears	"The New Digital Divide: Overcoming Online Segregation," *Sojourners Magazine*, January 2009.
Larry Seltzer	"Wireless Access: The Next Great Municipal Crisis," *eWeek*, June 23, 2005.

Index

C

D

E

Y